Access to History

John Calvin and the
Later Reformation

Access to History

General Editor: Keith Randell

John Calvin and the Later Reformation

Keith Randell

Hodder & Stoughton

A MEMBER OF THE HODDER HEADLINE GROUP

The cover illustration is a portrait of John Calvin in later life
(Courtesy University of Geneva)

Some other titles in the series:

Luther and the German Reformation, 1517–55
Keith Randell ISBN 0 340 51808 1
The Catholic and Counter Reformations
Keith Randell ISBN 0 340 53495 8
Spain, Rise and Decline, 1474–1643
Jill Kilsby ISBN 0 340 51807 3
Charles V, Ruler, Dynast and Defender of the Faith
Stewart MacDonald ISBN 0 340 53558 X
From Revolt to Independence: The Netherlands 1550–1650
Martyn Rady ISBN 0 340 51803 0
The Unification of Germany 1815–90
Andrina Stiles ISBN 0 340 51810 3
The Unification of Italy 1815–70
Andrina Stiles ISBN 0 340 51809 X

British Library Cataloguing in Publication Data

Randell, Keith
  Calvin and the Later Reformation
  (Access to history)
  I. Reformed churches. Calvin, Jean, 1509-1564 – Biographies
  I. Title   II. Series 284′.2′0924

ISBN 0 340 52940 7

First published in Access to A-Level History series 1988
Impression number 10   9   8   7   6
Year   1998   1997   1996   1995   1994

Typeset by Photoprint, Torquay
Printed in Great Britain for Hodder & Stoughton Educational, a division of
Hodder Headline Plc, 338 Euston Road, London NW1 3BH
by Page Bros, Norwich

Contents

Preface

To the general reader

Although the *Access to History* series has been designed with the needs of students studying the subject at higher examination levels very much in mind, it also has a great deal to offer the general reader. The main body of the text (i.e. ignoring the Study Guides at the ends of chapters) forms a readable and yet stimulating survey of a coherent topic as studied by historians. However, each author's aim has not merely been to provide a clear explanation of what happened in the past (to interest and inform): it has also been assumed that most readers wish to be stimulated into thinking further about the topic and to form opinions of their own about the significance of the events that are described and discussed (to be challenged). Thus, although no prior knowledge of the topic is expected on the reader's part, she or he is treated as an intelligent and thinking person throughout. The author tends to share ideas and possibilities with the reader, rather than passing on numbers of so-called 'historical truths'.

To the student reader

There are many ways in which the series can be used by students studying History at a higher level. It will, therefore, be worthwhile thinking about your own study strategy before you start your work on this book. Obviously, your strategy will vary depending on the aim you have in mind, and the time for study that is available to you.

If, for example, you want to acquire a general overview of the topic in the shortest possible time, the following approach will probably be the most effective:

1. Read Chapter 1 and think about its contents.
2. Read the 'Making notes' section at the end of Chapter 2 and decide whether it is necessary for you to read this chapter.
3. If it is, read the chapter, stopping at each heading or ★ to note down the main points that have been made.
4. Repeat stage 2 (and stage 3 where appropriate) for all the other chapters.

If, however, your aim is to gain a thorough grasp of the topic, taking however much time is necessary to do so, you may benefit from carrying out the same procedure with each chapter, as follows:

1. Read the chapter as fast as you can, and preferably at one sitting.
2. Study the flow diagram at the end of the chapter, ensuring that you understand the general 'shape' of what you have just read.

3. Read the 'Making notes' section (and the 'Answering essay questions' section, if there is one) and decide what further work you need to do on the chapter. In particularly important sections of the book, this will involve reading the chapter a second time and stopping at each heading and * to think about (and to write a summary of) what you have just read.
4. Attempt the 'Source-based questions' section. It will sometimes be sufficient to think through your answers, but additional understanding will often be gained by forcing yourself to write them down.

When you have finished the main chapters of the book, study the 'Further Reading' section and decide what additional reading (if any) you will do on the topic.

This book has been designed to help make your studies both enjoyable and successful. If you can think of ways in which this could have been done more effectively, please write to tell me. In the meantime, I hope that you will gain greatly from your study of History.

Keith Randell

CHAPTER 1

Introduction: John Calvin

John Calvin was the leading figure of the second half of the Reformation. He founded the strand of Protestantism – Calvinism – which breathed new life into the movement after the initial impetus provided by Martin Luther had largely been lost as Lutheranism became the safe new orthodoxy of most of northern Germany and Scandinavia. Calvinism, in contrast, was anything but safe. It required of its followers such a degree of commitment in all aspects of life that considerable political, social and economic changes normally followed its adoption. It was widely feared by those in authority in areas where it had not yet taken hold and its further spread was often fiercely resisted. Yet it successfully established itself in states and communities from Switzerland to Scotland, and was even responsible for the colonisation of some of the less hospitable parts of the eastern coast of North America. It retained its vitality for a century or more.

Some historians have gone as far as claiming that, without Calvin, the Reformation would probably have died and been largely forgotten. They see him as bringing purpose and coherence to a movement that had been given an explosive start by Luther, but which had then been allowed to fall under the domination of German princes who were more interested in securing their own social and political positions than in understanding God and His will. Although this view is by no means universally accepted, there is general agreement that Calvin was the one man among the 'second wave' of religious reformers who was capable of taking hold of the Reformation and re-directing it along paths that would ensure its continued growth and development. In the process of doing so, he established for himself a place in History that is scarcely less prominent than that of Luther. Certainly, writers have been intrigued for centuries by the similarities and differences between these two men whose lives and work so extensively overlapped, but who never actually met.

John Calvin was a Frenchman, born at Noyon in Picardy in 1509. His name was Jean Chauvin, but like many aspiring scholars of the time, he adopted the Latinised name of Calvinus as a young man. His father was a lawyer who had secured for himself important local legal positions within the Church. He was ambitious for his son, whom he hoped would continue the family's rise from social obscurity, and he did everything possible to ensure that this would happen. He placed his son to be brought up in the household of the leading local family, so that he would learn the etiquette of the well-to-do and form the contacts that should be of advantage to him in later life. He assumed that he would be able to obtain an opening for Jean within the priesthood of the

Church, so he started his son on the route taken by all non-aristocratic aspirants to Church preferment – the study of Latin and early entry to university. Jean turned out to be an outstanding scholar who quickly grew to love the mental gymnastics through which he was led. But he was totally unquestioning of the future his father had mapped out for him. When, for some reason that is not known for certain, his father decided that his son's future was to be in the law and not in the Church, Calvin obediently transferred to another university so that he could study law rather than theology.

Calvin was still studying law when his father died in 1531. The detail of what took place over the next few years is largely unknown. The evidence that remains is very partial and is, in some respects, contradictory. It is certain that he abandoned the law and returned to the study of Latin and Greek, which seem to have been his first love. He appears to have been particularly attracted to the writings of the Ancients, the pre-Christian literary figures of Greece and Rome. He even paid to have his commentary on one of them published. He also seems to have become interested in Protestantism for the first time, although it is impossible to date or explain the change with precision. The evidence we have is that he fled from the harshly orthodox University of Paris in late 1533 because he was suspected of being a secret Protestant. His only explanation of this change from unthinking acceptance to outright rejection of the Church's position was made in Latin more than twenty years later and was generally unhelpful:

1 At first, I was so obstinately devoted to the superstitions of the
   Papacy (and more stubbornly so than was right for someone of my
   age) that I was not easily extricated from so profound an abyss.
   Then God, by a sudden conversion, changed and shaped my heart
5 towards being more receptive. Having received some foretaste of
   true godliness I at once burned with so great a zeal to progress
   that although I did not give up my other studies I yet pursued
   them more slackly . . .

There has been an enormous amount of speculation by Calvin's many biographers in an attempt to explain why the brilliant scholar, who had previously shown no compelling interest in religion, should have risked his position by espousing a cause that was treated with great suspicion by the authorities in France at the time. Sometimes this has been done by assuming that some of his writings were autobiographical, although there is no direct evidence that they were. One extract that has been much used as a source of explanation was in fact claimed by Calvin to be imaginary. At best, it might show what he liked to think happened to him: more probably it was a device used to persuade loyal Catholics that their reservations about abandoning their faith were quite natural.

1 The more closely I examined myself, the sharper became the
stings of conscience which pricked me, so much so that my only
relief lay in deceiving myself and forgetting about it . . . Then,
however, there arose another form of doctrine which was not to
5 turn away from the profession of Christianity but to take it back
to its own source and to restore it, cleansed of all its corruptions,
to its essential purity. Offended by this novel notion, at first I
listened reluctantly to it and, I must confess, resisted it with
strength and vigour. It is natural to be stubborn and obstinate and
10 continue in a predetermined course of action and I was only
persuaded with the greatest difficulty to confess that I had been in
ignorance and error all my life.

Tempting as it is to believe that here is the perfect explanation of
Calvin's conversion, the truth is that we shall never know with any
degree of certainty exactly what happened. This is in stark contrast
with the well-documented mental and emotional anguish suffered by
Martin Luther. (Comparisons with Luther, made throughout this
book, can be followed up in *Luther and the German Reformation* in this
series.)

After fleeing from Paris in late 1533, Calvin seems to have expected
to be able to continue his studies in peace under the protection of highly
placed Protestant friends in the provinces. This he did for about a year,
but he decided to leave the country when the authorities launched a
campaign to identify and arrest heretics however influential they might
be. His choice of Basel, in Switzerland, as a refuge was not accidental.
It was the virtually independent city to which many of his friends had
already escaped. The fact that it was a centre of moderate opposition to
the Church suggests that Calvin was in no sense an extremist at this
stage in his religious development. Nor was he expecting to take any
leading role in events. He merely wished to be able to continue his
researches and writings without having his life threatened.

He was able to remain in Basel long enough to complete his first
Protestant book. *Christianae Religionis Institutio* (*The Institutes of the
Christian Religion*) was written in Latin. It was essentially a summary of
the major Protestant beliefs, and it immediately marked Calvin out as
an organised and clear thinker of the highest calibre. The *Institutio*
became one of the most influential books of the Reformation, although
not in its original 1536 edition. It was revised and massively enlarged
throughout Calvin's lifetime and succeeding editions, in both Latin and
French, provided the clearest available statement of what should be
believed and why.

It seemed that Calvin had joined the growing number of Protestant
scholars who lived nomadic existences, travelling from city to city in
search of a safe haven where their views would be acceptable. But his
wanderings were temporarily halted by the appeals made to his

conscience during a chance overnight stay at Geneva in August 1536. The city was in a state of some confusion. It was a large (population c.10,000) and independent city which traditionally had been ruled over by its Prince-Bishop, although it had fallen within the territories controlled by the Dukes of Savoy (see map on page 5). But for some years, a number of the citizens had seen the possibility of greater independence in breaking these links and developing ties with the neighbouring Swiss Confederation. These political aspirations had gained an additional dimension with the advent of the Reformation. For many people, the struggle against the Bishop's party had now become an issue of religious principle, rather than the pursuit of self-interest. The Protestants were in the ascendancy in 1536, although the struggle was by no means over. On hearing that the author of *Christianae Religionis Institutio* was in the city, Guillaume Farel, the leader of the Protestant cause, tried every conceivable argument to persuade him to stay and to lend his support. Twenty years later Calvin described what happened:

1 . . . the city was divided into ungodly and dangerous factions . . . Farel, who was consumed with an extraordinary zeal to advance the gospel, immediately strained every nerve to detain me. And, after learning that my heart was set upon devoting myself to
5 private studies, for which I wished to keep myself free from other pursuits, and, finding that he achieved nothing by his entreaties, he proceeded to warn me that God would curse my retirement and the tranquillity which I sought for my studies if I withdrew and refused to help when it was so urgently needed . . . I felt as if
10 God from Heaven had laid his mighty hand upon me to detain me. By this I was so struck with terror that I gave up the journey I had planned to undertake. But, aware of my natural shyness, I refused to tie myself to any particular position.

So began an association with Geneva that was to be central to Calvin's work for the remaining 28 years of his life. It has frequently been stated that the situation he found in the city was likely to make the most of his strengths and minimise his weaknesses. For Calvin was not a great innovator or motivator. He could not have done what Luther did in Germany between 1517 and 1520, when he launched the Reformation by acting as an emotional and intellectual focal point for those who were prepared to question the prevailing orthodoxy. It is tempting, but an overstatement, to suggest that Calvin never had an original thought. But it would be fair to maintain that he was at his best when he could take up the work begun by others and further advance it by thinking it through to its logical conclusion and by organising and administering it with great efficiency. His talents were outstanding in terms of drive and determination and intellectual and organisational ability, but not as a

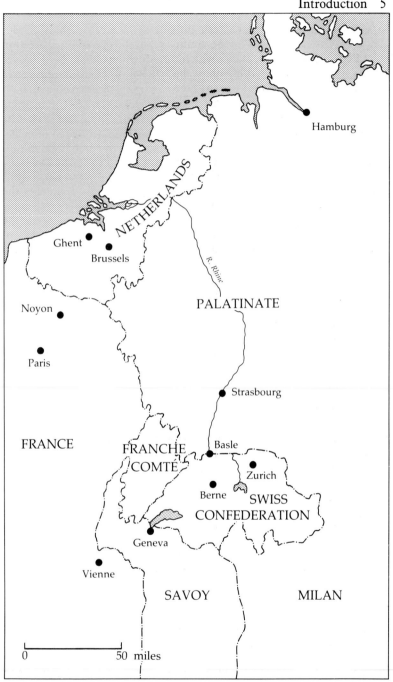

Geneva and her neighbours in the mid-sixteenth century

generator of new ideas. He was therefore in many ways the ideal person to take the myriad disparate attempts at Church reform that had been made during the previous twenty years, and marshal them into a coherent structure that would ensure that the enthusiasm and energy of the early reformers would not be lost with the passage of time.

The fact that Calvin saw himself as serving God's will by remaining in Geneva was to have a dramatic effect on what happened. Had he been merely following his own inclinations, perhaps in search of power or prestige, he would not have been possessed by that unassailable certainty of the correctness of his ideas and actions which was to characterise his behaviour. Even more so than Luther, who was at least prepared to approach some issues with an open mind, Calvin believed that the people who challenged or disagreed with him were the agents of the Devil. Because he has traditionally been viewed as living his life with little outward show of emotion, and as being devoid of the common human faults and frailties, he has tended to be thought of as a somewhat forbidding figure whom it would have been easier to respect than to like. Numbers of his biographers have attempted to show that there were human sides to the archetypal 'man of God', but they generally carry little conviction. It has to be admitted that few people found him an attractive personality. Many would argue that it was because of this – rather than despite this – that he had such a great effect on History. The story of this effect and the ways in which it was achieved provides the unifying element in the chapters that follow.

Making notes on '*Introduction: John Calvin*'

The purpose of this brief introductory chapter is to set something of the scene for the rest of the book. You are unlikely ever to use the information it contains in an examination situation. But you will need to carry forward the understandings you have acquired, so that you can make sense of what follows. To find out whether or not you have understood the main points of this chapter, look quickly at each paragraph and write a short sentence summarising its main point. You should find that your nine sentences form a logical sequence of ideas.

Source-based questions on '*Introduction: John Calvin*'

1 Calvin's conversion
Read the two extracts from Calvin's writings given on pages 2 and 3. Answer the following questions:
a) What is meant in the second extract by 'to take it back to its own source' (line 5)?
b) What evidence of hostility to the Catholic Church does the first

extract contain? What does the lack of such hostility in the second
extract suggest?
c) What does the first sentence of the first extract imply about the
involvement of other people in Calvin's conversion?
d) What – assuming that both extracts relate to Calvin and are
accurate – were the stages in his conversion?
e) What are the strengths and weaknesses of these extracts as
evidence about Calvin's conversion?

2 Calvin's decision to remain in Geneva in 1536
Read the extract from Calvin's writings, given on page 4 and answer
the following questions:
a) What is meant by 'to advance the gospel' (line 2)?
b) What evidence is there that Farel was desperate for Calvin to
remain in Geneva? Why might this have been?
c) What does the extract suggest about Calvin's personality and
beliefs?
d) What factors should be considered when evaluating the reliability
of this extract as evidence of Calvin's motives for remaining in
Geneva?

CHAPTER 2

Calvin and Geneva: The Early Years

1 Introduction

The story of Calvin's long love-hate relationship with the city of Geneva has all the makings of a popular drama series for television. It is no wonder that it has fascinated historians. Many of Calvin's biographers have devoted most of the space available to them to recreating the dramatic happenings that for so long appeared to be leading to disaster, but which then unexpectedly turned into a major success. Many students of History have had their imaginations fired by the struggle for mastery that took place in the remote lake-side city on the frontiers of the French and German-speaking worlds.

It is understandable that the 'events' of Calvin's life should have been the focus of many writers' attention. After all, it is often the well-told story that first awakens interest in history, and which helps to create patterns of the past in people's minds. Before judgements about the success and influence of a person, and the reasons for it, can be made, a clear outline understanding of what is thought to have happened is needed. This can best be gained from a narrative account. But in following the narrative it is desirable to keep in mind the 'issues' that make the story significant. What is it that makes the study of the life of this person worthwhile historically?

In Calvin's case the answers are mainly concerned with his wider influence. They have to do with identifying the factors that led to him becoming the most influential figure of the Reformation for people outside Germany. But they also involve considerations of establishing 'historical truth'. Calvin has been more maligned by his opponents and more adulated by his supporters than most historical characters, and there is a need to attempt to determine wherein lies the truth. In particular, there is the necessity to reach conclusions about the nature of this man who has been variously portrayed as being monster and saint. The study of Calvin's life in Geneva yields many insights into these issues, especially as the events are particularly well documented for the time – in marked contrast with the earlier years of his life where it is possible to be certain about very little.

* With hindsight it is possible to identify three distinct periods in Calvin's life in Geneva. The first period was brief, less than two years, and ended with his expulsion from the city in April 1538. The second period was long (and arduous), lasting from September 1541, when he

See Preface for explanation of * symbol.

agreed to return to Geneva, to June 1555 when the last of his powerful opponents were defeated. This was the time of constant struggle when it frequently seemed that his efforts would come to nought and that any 'advances' that had been made would be lost. The third period, from June 1555 until his death in April 1564, was the time of triumph. For these years his influence was unchallenged and his advice was generally followed. Geneva became the Calvinist community of tradition.

2 Geneva

For the story of Calvin's struggles to be properly understood, it must be firmly rooted in the political and social context of this most unusual city, whose development in the sixteenth century ran counter to the general western European trend. In an era when city after city was surrendering its freedoms to the local ruler (whether prince or monarch), Geneva established itself as an independent republic and maintained its independence against all challenges. It was not until 1798 that it fell under the control of one of its 'mighty' neighbours, in this case Napoleonic France. Nor, in Calvin's lifetime, did it become a republic in name only, as happened with many of the surviving city republics that were dominated by a single family which in practice exercised princely rule. This was highly significant because it meant that, in Geneva, power was shared widely, making it difficult to bring about change. In an era when there were no political parties in the modern sense of being subject to party discipline, the only way to secure change was to win over a very large number of individuals. Even when this had been done, the position was not secure as a decision made at one meeting was likely to be reversed at the next meeting in a fresh vote called by those who had had second thoughts.

The structure for decision-making within the city was complex. Most power lay with the Little Council, made up of 25 men who were elected annually by the Council of Two Hundred, the next most important body. The Little Council met several times each week and dealt with matters of day-to-day business, as well as framing major policy proposals that were taken to the Council of Two Hundred for its agreement. Most of the leading citizens were fairly routinely elected to the Little Council, a sign of their social eminence, and they expected the Council of Two Hundred to follow their lead. This normally happened – whenever the Little Council was united in its view. But when the Little Council was divided, as often happened when Calvin was involved, the Two Hundred became of great importance. This meant that there were large numbers of decision-makers to be influenced.

The framers of the Republic's constitution had taken care to safeguard against power falling into a few hands. For instance, they ensured that many families were represented on the Little Council by

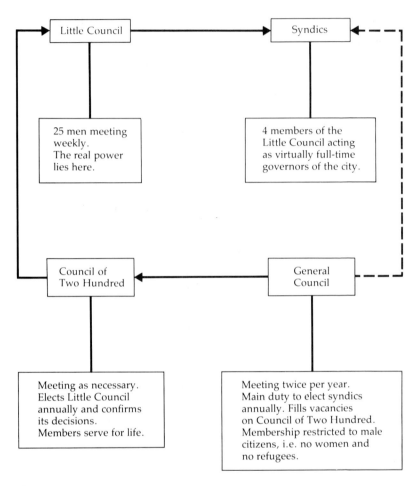

The government of Geneva in the mid-sixteenth century

stipulating that father and son, or brother and brother, could not serve in the same year. However, the effective leadership of the city was given to a small group, four Syndics, who were elected annually by the General Council of all male citizens. But they were not allowed consecutive years in office, so they could not build themselves a permanent power base. Yet the Syndics were very influential people. They were living symbols of the authority of the Republic, and their orders were not to be disobeyed with impunity. Nor were their opinions easily challenged. So it was difficult to introduce change without their active support, just as it was necessary to ensure the support of a majority of the Little Council and the acquiescence of the Two Hundred.

* Further complications were added to this complex political situation by the existence of long-running controversies in Geneva. This led to the formation of political factions which were in such fierce rivalry with one another that they were unprepared to agree about anything, unless they could see that the price to be paid for continued disagreement was very high. What was worse, Calvin and his cause became identified with one of the factions. This was partly unavoidable. Although the people of Geneva spoke French, they no more regarded themselves as being French than English-speaking Welshmen think of themselves as being English. One of the Genevan factions was pro-French, seeing the King of France as a suitable protector against the Duke of Savoy who had sworn to regain control of the city and to re-incorporate it within his territories. This pro-French faction was linked in the public mind with support for the religious policies of the numerous French refugees, such as Calvin, who had fled from the spasmodic purges of Protestants ordered by Francis I. Therefore those who opposed the idea of an alliance with France tended to be hostile to Calvin, seeing that there was political capital to be made by obstructing him. They could be sure of a sympathetic hearing from many native-born Genevans who were brought up on an unthinking dislike of the French, to which was added a genuine fear of being swamped by the refugees who arrived in such great numbers that at times it seemed as if they were almost in a majority. Thus, merely because he was French, Calvin was certain to experience an amount of opposition.

Luckily for Calvin, the other faction also had natural disadvantages. It liked to project itself as the patriotic party, saving Geneva from unwanted French influence. But it had to look for support from somewhere, as it was obvious that the city could not resist Savoy unaided, despite the fact that it was protected by massive city walls. This faction advocated a strengthening of the ties with Berne, with whom Geneva had been allied since the beginnings of the struggle with Savoy in 1526. This could have been a popular move because Berne was also a Protestant state, but problems were caused by the fact that Berne made little secret of her desire to dominate Geneva rather than to protect her independence. Whenever Berne was particularly grasping in her dealings with her ally, the pro-Berne faction became unpopular and the pro-French faction was given a situation to exploit. None of this, of course, had anything to do with the merits or demerits of Calvin's case, but it was to play a significant part in determining the degree of his success.

3 The First Attempt

When Calvin reluctantly agreed to remain in Geneva and to help Farel in his work of consolidating the Reformation in the city, he was awarded no official capacity. Farel was clearly the religious leader of the community, and Calvin was merely one of his unofficial assistants. The combination of talents was theoretically a good one. Farel was older and more experienced, with the proven ability to inspire audiences and to whip up religious fervour. Calvin was intellectually much more able and was a natural organiser, as he had already shown in his *Christianae Religionis Institutio*. But the new team had very real problems. At this stage in their lives, neither member had any political sense. They were both men with a mission, who did not believe in compromise. They each had a clear understanding of what they took to be God's will, and they were determined to do their best to implement it. They gave no thought to what was possible, given the divisions and tensions that existed within the city. It is little wonder that Farel and Calvin soon found themselves in an untenable position.

This, of course, is not to imply that they had a favourable situation with which to deal. Part of Farel's desperation in his appeals to Calvin to stay no doubt sprang from his recognition that current circumstances were very unpromising. Calvin summed up the environment he had entered when reminiscing on what he thought was his death bed:

> When I first came to this Church, I found nothing in it. There was preaching and that was all. They would look out for idols, it is true, and burn them. But there was no reformation; everything was in disorder.

If Calvin's many complaints made in private letters are accurate reflections of reality, the people of Geneva were particularly unspiritual. They had remained virtually untouched by the various revivals in religious feeling that had affected much of Europe in the previous half-century. What had taken place since the ejection of the Bishop, largely on political grounds, in 1526 had been the 'negative' side of the Reformation. Old practices, such as the veneration of saints, fasting and the celebration of the Mass, had been discontinued, but little that was positive had been put in their place. Farel and his supporters had done their best to arouse the religious awareness of the people but with only limited success. Many citizens were unwilling to abandon old ways completely as they feared that eternal damnation might be their fate if they did. Others merely saw the changes in terms of the removal of irksome duties which left more time and money for enjoying themselves. Few had much understanding of what the Reformation really meant.

Calvin, like Farel, was so appalled by what he saw happening around him that he was certain of the need for radical and urgent action. He felt that both extensive education and firm discipline were required. The education could be provided through sermons in which God's wishes, as communicated through his Word, the Bible, could be explained. But the discipline, necessary to ensure that the people listened to the sermons and carried out what they had been told, could only be imposed with the support of the government – the Syndics and the Councils. So Farel and Calvin devoted most of their energy to preaching and attempting to persuade the governors of the city to take the drastic action they considered necessary.

* Much progress was actually made. The members of the Little Council were generally sympathetic to the aims of the reformers, and were eager to be taught what they should do. They were clearly impressed by Farel's and Calvin's knowledge and powers of persuasion, and were often prepared to take the action that was recommended by them. As a result, it was decided that all citizens should be required to swear adherence, in public, to a brief statement of belief that Calvin had drawn up. It was also agreed to implement, virtually unchanged, the *Articles on the Organisation of the Church and its Worship in Geneva* that Calvin wrote and Farel presented to the Council in January 1537. The *Articles* introduced the concept of discipline imposed by the use of excommunication, by which people guilty of actions that were contrary to the reformers' teachings would be barred from 'communing' with the faithful believers at the Lord's Supper (the replacement for the Mass). It was a written assumption of the *Articles* that the Council would wish to punish those whom the ministers chose to excommunicate.

* However, it soon became apparent that the task of persuading the Council was proceeding more speedily than the work of educating the people. Large numbers of citizens, including many of the most influential, failed to appear at the designated places and times to take their oath, and taunting Farel and Calvin in the streets became almost a popular sport among 'the lower orders'. In the face of such widespread and vocal opposition to the Reformers, the Council was only prepared to proceed slowly in forcing compliance with their instructions. This seemed like cowardice to Farel and Calvin, who were not slow in pointing out to the Council where its duty lay. They also caused great offence by showing that they regarded the Council as being, in essence, their servant, rather than the other way round. This the Council was not prepared to accept.

In 1538, Syndics were elected who were committed to the reformed religion, but who made a virtue of refusing to be dictated to by Farel and Calvin. The opportunity soon arose to test the issue of who were the leaders and who the led. Berne was attempting to introduce common practices into the various reformed churches that existed within its sphere of influence. The pro-Berne faction in Geneva favoured adoption of these common practices, especially as they were known to be against Farel and Calvin's teachings. The Council issued instructions that the Berne practices should be followed. Farel and Calvin not only refused, but went to the extreme lengths of excommunicating the whole city. The General Council's response was clear:

> 1 It was proposed that, if Calvin, Farel and any other preacher did not wish to obey the orders of the magistrates then it was a question whether they should continue in their posts which the General Council and the Little Council should vote upon. The
> 5 majority opinion was in favour of giving them the next three days to leave the city.

The Little Council was equally determined, and Farel and Calvin were expelled.

Few commentators at the time or subsequently have expressed much sympathy for the rejected reformers. They have been almost universally seen as being unreasonable, 'over-stepping the mark', failing to make allowances for human weaknesses, 'harsh and unbending', and totally lacking in political skill. It would be hard to disagree with the generality of such verdicts if one were using criteria that defined 'reasonableness' in terms of liberal-democratic values or in terms of likely practical outcomes. But if one were judging according to the values of the people who took the actions – as, some would argue, historians should – Farel and Calvin's actions were eminently reasonable. They believed that their duty was, like that of some of the Old Testament prophets, to proclaim God's Word to a 'lost' people, and to leave it to God to decide whether the Word would be listened to or not. They were in no sense responsible for the results of their actions: they merely had to do what they knew to be right. Such has been the reasoning of the totally committed person throughout the ages. The less committed describe such people as extremists, often prefixing the word 'dangerous' to their description. Certainly, in 1538 many Genevans regarded Farel and Calvin as dangerous extremists and they were pleased to see them go. But it did not mean that there was any thought of returning the city to obedience to Rome. It was just that the citizens wished for a less oppressive type of reformed religion.

4 Exile in Strasbourg

Farel and Calvin split up soon after leaving Geneva. Farel felt called to continue in the ministry and accepted an invitation to lead the Church in Neuchatel, another town that was loosely linked with the Swiss Confederation. Calvin, on the other hand, had been badly bruised by his Genevan experiences, and took his rejection to be a sign from God that his calling was to continue with the theological studies that had been so rudely interrupted. However, he reluctantly accepted urgent entreaties from Martin Bucer to come to Strasbourg in order to undertake a mixture of study and teaching duties.

At Strasbourg Calvin was initially employed as a lecturer on the Bible. But he was soon persuaded to act as the minister for the group of several hundred French exiles living in this German-speaking city. However, his main reason for being in Strasbourg was to work alongside Bucer. Bucer was one of the most respected Protestant leaders. He had remained independent of Luther, while agreeing with many of his teachings. Equally he had refused to become totally identified with Zwingli and the style of religion he introduced in Zurich. His main aim was to seek agreement between all committed Christians, including Catholics, and he remained optimistic that the Reformation would not result in permanent divisions within the Church. He was therefore energetic in his attempts to bring representatives of the various Protestant groups together with delegates from Rome in order to find a form of words that would be acceptable to both. He was not successful.

Calvin shared Bucer's belief that there could only be one Church. He even attended one of the sets of meetings at which it was hoped to reach agreement with the Catholics. But he was soon disillusioned by what he saw to be the unwillingness of the Catholics to admit to any of their errors. He remained convinced that there was only one true Church, but was now certain that the followers of the Pope could not be part of it. His increasing familiarity with the Bible and with the writings of the Early Fathers (the major theologians of the first centuries of Christianity), also convinced him that the teachings he had published in *Christianae Religionis Institutio* were correct. How much of this certainty was a result of contact with Bucer, who shared similar views on many matters of detail, is not known. Those historians who describe Calvin as being in Bucer's debt for many of his ideas have only circumstantial evidence to support their contention. It is more likely that Calvin was drawn to Bucer because of the similarity of their views, and that the influence of the established reformer was to act as a confirmer and clarifier of existing thoughts rather than as a major source of new ideas. Certainly the new and much enlarged version of *Christianae Religionis Institutio* that appeared in 1539 was a development of, rather than a replacement of, the teachings in the first edition.

* It seems that Calvin would have settled very happily in Strasbourg. He married, became a citizen, established himself as a renowned teacher to whom students were attracted, and found plenty of time to continue his studies. But he was not to remain undisturbed. The situation had changed dramatically in Geneva. The pro-Berne faction was in disgrace, with its leading members either executed for misdemeanours or in exile. The leaders of the pro-French faction that was now in control was seriously concerned that the ministers who had replaced Farel and Calvin were not of the quality required to convince the people of the need to alter their ways. The only person they knew of who possessed the necessary ability and commitment was Calvin. They

Portrait of John Calvin probably painted from life in the 1540s

decided to invite him back. But Calvin was most unwilling to go. It took a year of persuading, cajoling and promising to convince him that it was God's will that he abandon a life of contentment for one that seemed certain to be made up of constant aggravation. At last he gave way and accepted the invitation, deluding himself that it might only be for a six month period, on loan from Strasbourg! A special wagon was sent to collect him, his wife, her two children by a previous marriage, and his possessions. On 13 September 1541 he arrived in Geneva, and there he remained until his death 23 years later.

5 The Organisation of the Church

One of the promises that had been made to Calvin in order to secure his return was that urgent steps would be taken to arrange for the proper organisation of the Church in Geneva. And true to their word, the Little Council immediately appointed a small committee to work with him in drawing up the framework of the new structure. The task was completed within a fortnight, presumably with Calvin supplying all the ideas, and by the end of the year the resulting *Ecclesiastical Ordinances* had become law.

The *Ordinances* were entirely based on what Calvin believed to be God's will as expressed in the Bible. It has been argued that he merely copied what Bucer was attempting to introduce in Strasbourg, but this ignores the fact that all Calvin's teachings were soundly based on Biblical texts or the practices of the early Church. He never pretended that his ideas were original. In fact, just the opposite, as he always claimed to be restoring the purity of the true Church that had been lost over the centuries during which the Catholic Church, under the control of the Pope, had been perverted by a series of manmade laws. The fact that other reformers had come to similar conclusions earlier in no sense proves Calvin to be a plagiarist. He came to his own conclusions, based mainly on his reading of God's Word.

* Nonetheless, his understanding of God's wishes about the detail of the duties to be carried out by each of the four 'orders of offices' there were to be in the Church most probably gained directly from his contact with Bucer, who had come to similar conclusions. Gone was the élite of the priesthood with its special status dependent on its ability to forgive or to damn people on God's behalf. This, it was claimed, had been passed on from priest to priest starting with St Peter who in turn had received his powers directly from Jesus. In its place was to be a group of pastors (more often called ministers in English) whose main task was to be 'to proclaim the Word of God, to teach, admonish, exhort and reprove publicly and privately, to administer the sacraments and . . . to administer fraternal warnings'. There was to be no pretence that the ministers had a special relationship with God: they were ordinary people who had been chosen to do this work because they possessed the necessary qualities.

* Calvin clearly intended to do away with the rigid distinction between the civil power (the government and its agencies) and the

spiritual power (the Church). This distinction, which the Papacy still struggled to maintain, was to Calvin another perversion that had arisen since the days of the early Church. He saw government as being indivisible. The duty of the churchman and the magistrate (anyone with civil power) was to work in unison to bring about God's will. Thus considerable influence over the Church was to be given to lay people, in order to bring about the real partnership that God wanted to exist. This was mainly to be done through the 'order' of the elders. The elders were to be men with no particular training who were chosen because they lived 'good' lives. Their duty was 'to supervise every person's conduct. In friendly fashion they should warn backsliders and those of disorderly life. After that, where necessary, they should report to the ministers

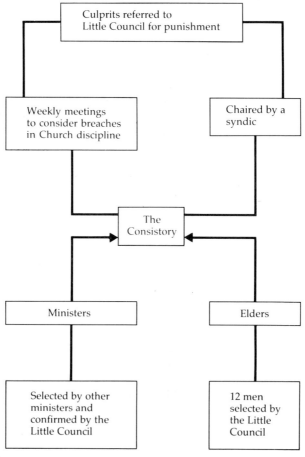

Church government in Calvin's Geneva

who will arrange for fraternal correction'. In Geneva there were to be 12 elders drawn from all parts of the city, so that everybody's activities could be kept under close scrutiny.

* The power of the elders was to come from the fact that they were in a majority in the ruling body of the Church – the Consistory. The Consistory, made up of the ministers and the elders, was to meet once a week:

1 to ensure that there is no disorder in the Church and to discuss together any necessary remedial action. Since they have neither the power nor the authority to use force, we have agreed to assign one of our officials to them to summon those whom they wish to
5 admonish. If any one should deliberately refuse to appear, the Council is to be informed so as to take action. If any one teaches things contrary to the received doctrine he shall be summoned to a conference. If he listens to reason, let him be sent back without any scandal or disgrace. If he is obstinate, he should be
10 admonished several times until it is apparent that greater severity is needed: then he shall be forbidden to attend the Lord's Supper and he shall be reported to the magistrates.

If any one fails to come to church to such a degree that there is real dislike for the community of believers manifested, or if any
15 one shows that he cares nothing for ecclesiastical order, let him be admonished, and if he be tractable let him be amicably sent back. If however he goes from bad to worse, after having been warned three times, let him be cut off from the Church and be denounced to the magistrate.

The other two 'orders', the doctors and the deacons, were to play no part in implementing the discipline of the Church. Their roles were merely to serve, the doctors as teachers 'to instruct the faithful in sound doctrine so that the purity of the gospel is not corrupted by ignorance or wrong opinion', and the deacons to administer the collection and distribution of money for the sick and the poor. But they are important in illustrating the coherence of Calvin's scheme. It is difficult, in an age when management skills are so advanced and widely practised, to appreciate how chaotic most public life in the sixteenth century was. Even in the government of the most powerful states there was often considerable confusion about who did what, and systems and structures were generally ill-defined and based on customs that could be contra-dictory. Geneva, for instance, had no written constitution until Calvin, at the request of the Council, drafted one for them, and in the process eliminated numbers of inconsistencies. It is therefore unsurprising that Calvin should have become renowned as a creator of systems – an outstanding organiser in a period when such people were rare – because the *Ecclesiastical Ordinances* represent an attempt to erect a structure of

all-pervading responsibilities that was unique in its completeness in Reformation Europe.
* However, the *Ordinances* did not become law just as Calvin wrote them. By comparing the original draft with the final version, it is possible to speculate on what probably happened. Calvin was still somewhat naive, despite his previous experiences in Geneva, about the willingness of the Council to share its authority. He assumed that in a situation where all parties desired the same outcome, power could be shared amicably. The members of the Council did not agree. They were determined to maintain their position as the ultimate authority in all matters and as the only body in Geneva able to punish citizens and other inhabitants. So, at vital points throughout Calvin's draft, words and phrases were added to the *Ordinances* to strengthen the Council's position. Elders were to be 'nominated and appointed by the government'; new ministers were still to be recommended to the Council by the existing ministers, but were to be accepted by the Council 'as it thinks fit'; and, when there was any disagreement over doctrine, experts from outside Geneva 'appointed by the government' were to be called in to help resolve the dispute. But, most significantly of all, a whole paragraph was added to the section dealing with the Consistory:

> 1 All this must be done in such a way that the ministers have no civil jurisdiction nor use anything but the spiritual sword of the word of God as St Paul commands them; nor is the authority of the Consistory to diminish in any way that of the magistrate or
> 5 ordinary justice. The civil power must remain unimpaired. In cases where, in future, there may be need to impose punishments or constrain individuals, then the ministers and the Consistory, having heard the case and used such admonitions and exhortations as are appropriate, should report the whole matter to the
> 10 Council which, in turn, will judge and sentence according to the needs of the case.

Yet, despite the changes made to the original draft by the Council, the *Ecclesiastical Ordinances* of 1541 was in many ways a remarkable document. For the first time a complete and coherent structure for the organisation and government of a Protestant Church had been laid down. And the quality of the work that Calvin had done was very high, giving ample evidence of the success of his training as a lawyer. As a result, the Genevan model was so difficult to improve upon, if the aim was to mirror the early Church and the declared wishes of Jesus as closely as possible, that it was widely copied by Reformed churches throughout the Christian world.
A very significant aspect of the *Ordinances* was the huge amount of power and responsibility that lay with the ministers even after the

changes made by the Council. In the Lutheran states of Germany and Zwinglian states of Switzerland, the Church was clearly subservient to the government in almost all matters. This, it could be argued, was one of the main reasons why Protestantism was so immediately appealing to many of the princes of Germany. This makes the Genevan situation even more remarkable, especially when the sensitivity of the Council over this issue is taken into account. Calvin was not allowed all that he wanted, but he was able to win a fair proportion of it. The definition of doctrine (the beliefs of the Church) was essentially in the hands of the ministers, as was the ability to interfere in the daily lives of others through the large degree of influence they exercised in the Consistory. This influence extended to the Council chamber where the ministers were always assured of a hearing, and where Calvin could always remind the councillors that he had not asked to return to Geneva and could leave if they were not prepared to carry out God's will. This ability to exert pressure on the Council, although not written specifically into the *Ordinances*, was apparent from the whole tone of the document which indicated that the ministers would identify the wishes of God and would expect the Council to implement them. There was, however, no machinery for dealing with a situation in which the Council failed to match up to the ministers' expectations.

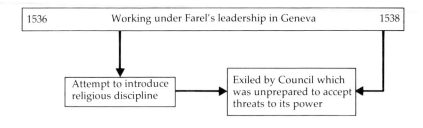

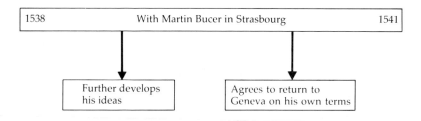

Summary – Calvin and Geneva: The Early Years

Making notes on 'Calvin and Geneva: The Early Years'

In making notes on this chapter you should concentrate on reaching understanding of three general areas. Firstly you should establish in your mind the 'shape' of the years 1536–64, and the features that typified each period. Then you should attempt to understand the political structure of Geneva and the ways in which this affected Calvin. Finally you should form a clear understanding of the way in which the Church in Geneva was organised, and why. The following headings, subheadings and questions should help you through this process.

1.   Introduction
1.1.   Why study what happened?
1.2.   The three periods
2.   Geneva
2.1.   The political structure (the Little Council, the Council of Two Hundred, and the Syndics)
2.2.   The factions. How did their existence affect Calvin?
3.   The First Attempt
3.1.   The situation in 1536
3.2.   Church organisation. What does this show of Calvin's aims and methods?
3.3.   Expulsion. How far was Calvin to blame?
4.   Exile in Strasbourg
4.1.   The influence of Bucer
4.2.   The return to Geneva. How did the circumstances of the return strengthen Calvin's position?
5.   The organisation of the Church
5.1.   The *Ecclesiastical Ordinances*
5.2.   The ministers
5.3.   The elders
5.4.   The Consistory
5.5.   The balance of power. How far was the Church in charge of its own affairs?

Source-based questions on 'Calvin and Geneva: The Early Years'

1 The exile of Farel and Calvin from Geneva, 1538
Read carefully the extract from the General Council's *Minutes*, given on page 14. Answer the following questions:
a) What was the *decision* made by the General Council? Was this likely to be a final decision?
b) What does the writer of the extract consider to be the issue of principle that was in dispute?

c) What impression of the General Council's attitude is given by the choice of 'the next three days' (line 5)?

d) To what extent is it possible to identify the point of view of the writer of the extract?

e) How far were Farel and Calvin to blame for their exile?

2 The Consistory

Read carefully the two extracts from the *Ecclesiastical Ordinances* given on pages 19 and 20. Answer the following questions:

a) In the first extract, what types of 'disorder' is it envisaged that the consistory will correct?

b) What stages is the consistory expected to go through in dealing with an offender?

c) Are the two extracts consistent in what they say or imply about the use of excommunication? Explain your answer.

d) Describe the *style* of discipline envisaged in the first extract. Support your answer with evidence.

e) What is the implication of the phrase 'judge and sentence according to the needs of the case' (lines 10–11) in the second extract?

f) Why was the Consistory likely to become unpopular? Could this have been avoided?

CHAPTER 3

Calvin and Geneva: Struggle and Victory

1 Struggles with the Opposition

If Calvin experienced any feelings of elation when the *Ordinances* became law in November 1541, he was soon to be disappointed. Ahead of him lay nearly fourteen years of struggle where he met opposition and obstruction at every turn. One problem was a continuation of the situation that had existed during his first period in Geneva, in that the various political factions used religion as an issue from which they could gain political advantage. So once again Calvin became the victim of campaigns against the amount of influence foreigners enjoyed in the city, especially when he could be accused of attempting to undermine the traditional Genevan patterns of life. He also had to contend with the widespread opposition provoked by the Consistory's close scrutiny of people's lives, public and private, for there were few who initially supported the level of detailed supervision that he thought was necessary. He was also plagued with difficulties over the interpretation of the *Ordinances*. It has been suggested that the wording used to describe excommunication, and who had the power to pronounce it, was left deliberately vague in order to secure its acceptance by the Council, and that from the outset both parties (the ministers and the Council) believed that the power rested with them. This interpretation is supported by circumstantial evidence in that Calvin utilised similar tactics when seeking agreement on doctrine with the Protestant churches of Switzerland (see page 81). This, of course, is not to deny the likelihood that some councillors made use of other possible interpretations of the wording of the *Ordinances* merely in order to embarrass him.

The types of opposition that Calvin faced were difficult for him to overcome. He was sniped at, taunted, made to wait, left unsupported in awkward situations, and forced to make an issue of what should have been straightforward. Seldom was he openly confronted. As a result he was constantly shooting at a moving target. Rarely was there a clearcut case for him to fight, and when there was, he was subjected to extreme delaying tactics before his demands were met. In these circumstances it may seem strange that he was neither driven out again, nor chose to leave of his own accord. But neither side wished to part company: they merely wanted the relationship to be managed on their own terms. The leading opponents were well aware of the strength of Calvin's position as an internationally famous reformer who was widely respected. It would do Geneva's reputation no good to be known as the city that had twice dispensed with the great man's services. In any case, most leading Genevans were convinced that Calvin was generally right. They just wished that he would not always push matters to their logical conclusion. If he had been somewhat more moderate in his demands of people, recognising that it is not reasonable to expect such high standards from everyone, they would have willingly co-operated with him.

Calvin, on the other hand, was overwhelmingly motivated to carry out what he thought was God's plan for him. Although he set off from Strasbourg claiming that his stay in Geneva would probably be temporary, by the time his wagon arrived at its destination he had convinced himself that God required him to serve in Geneva for the rest of his life, and he promised the Council that he would never desert them. His resolve was sorely tried on many occasions, and by 1554 he was fast nearing the stage where he was prepared to interpret his many reverses as a sign that God did not wish him to continue. But, although he sometimes weakened, he never surrendered. He displayed the highest order of dedication, perseverance and patience; despite the fact that his hot temper resulted in numerous bouts of public anger, he was always prepared to wait longer for success in the belief that 'God's will will be done'.

* All these years were difficult, but the late 1540s and early 1550s were particularly distressing. During this period, a group of men who were particularly hostile to him, led by Ami Perrin, were in control of the city. Perrin was the only Genevan of the period who was in any sense a match for Calvin. He was soundly based socially and politically, being the head of one of the city's leading families, with links by marriage to most of the other families of importance. But he was also a man of personality, presence and intelligence who generally used his position to advantage. He started as a firm supporter of Calvin, having been instrumental in securing the reformer's return, but he gradually became disenchanted as Calvin continued to show that he was no respecter of persons and that no deference would be shown to the rich and powerful. Perrin's position would have been unassailable had he been prepared to settle for what he had. But he wanted more, and may even have harboured hopes of establishing himself as the 'dictator' of the city. Having built up a position where he was clearly the most powerful man in the city he left himself vulnerable to attack by colleagues who resented his pre-eminence. He engaged in secret diplomacy with the King of France, seemingly with the intention of gaining a personal advantage, and when news of his activities leaked out his explanations lacked conviction. He also appeared to be setting himself and his family above the law when he supported his wife, who was at times a hysterical opponent of Calvin, in her refusal to accept correction from the Consistory.

Yet even with these mistakes, Perrin and his faction (known as the

Libertines) did not seem to be in danger of losing control of the situation. There was still widespread dislike of French refugees, especially as fresh influxes of them threatened to bring about a major housing shortage in the city, and the prying interference of the Consistory was even more resented than were the pretensions of Perrin and his family. A winning position was turned into a losing position by the events surrounding the Michael Servetus affair of 1553.

2 Michael Servetus

The Servetus affair was the most bizarre event with which Calvin was associated. Ever since it took place there has been controversy about what Calvin did or did not do, what were or were not his motives, and what the affair shows us of the reformer's personality and human qualities. Even now it is not possible to be certain about many of the details, and about the light that the events throw upon Calvin. But there is no disagreement over some of the salient points of the saga.

Michael Servetus was a Spaniard who had briefly been a monk before entering the university world in France and Germany as a man of great talent. However, he suffered from delusions of intellectual grandeur and his arrogance was monumental. He found it impossible to accept that his radical theological thinking was incorrect, even though he was unable to convince anybody of note of its validity. He expected to be treated as an equal by the outstanding theologians of the time, including Calvin, and became most offensive when he thought he was being patronised or undervalued. Nowadays he would probably be described as being mentally disturbed. Calvin was one of those who was subjected to unsolicited letters from Servetus requesting support and guidance, and whose attempts to be helpful were flung back in his face once it became clear that there was to be plenty of guidance but no support for his ideas. In particular, Servetus's determination to challenge the beliefs about the nature of the Trinity (the miracle by which God could be three – Father, Son and Holy Ghost – and one at the same time) which were central to Christianity, Catholic and Protestant, made his approaches distasteful. To those who regarded themselves as being orthodox Christians, Servetus was totally unacceptable, a dangerous heretic. He was especially repugnant to Calvin, for reasons that have never been clear, but which might have to do with the fact that they probably knew each other in their student days.

Servetus was a liar and a coward as well as being full of conceit. When, in the 1530s, his theological views attracted adverse attention, he disappeared from view, assumed a false identity and resurfaced as the medical adviser to the Archbishop of Vienne, in eastern France, where he thought he could escape the consequences of his heresy. Here he lived a counterfeit life as an orthodox Catholic, while continuing to develop his ideas on the Trinity. In early 1553 he arranged for the publication, anonymously and in great secrecy, of an updated version of his writings. But, although he went to great lengths to cover his tracks locally, he could not resist sending copies of his book to famous theologians such as Calvin. This proved his undoing. Calvin was so incensed at Servetus's renewed attempt to win support for his views that he allowed one of his followers to inform the French authorities that the innocent-seeming physician in Vienne was none other than the notorious Michael Servetus. Servetus was arrested but might have lied his way out of the situation had not Calvin produced written evidence that he was not telling the truth. The story seemed to be at an end when Servetus contrived to escape from his prison in Vienne, and was condemned to be burnt in effigy in his absence.

To the amazement of all who knew about the case, Servetus was spotted a short time later attending one of Calvin's sermons in Geneva. It seemed that his arrogance had turned to foolhardiness. He was immediately arrested, and at Calvin's insistence, was put on trial for attempting to lead others into heresy by publishing his erroneous views. But the case against him was not straightforward, especially when Servetus, learning of the strength of the opposition to Calvin within the city, went on to the offensive and began to frame eloquent and cogent arguments against Calvin's teachings. Perrin and the other leading Libertines saw this as an excellent opportunity to discredit Calvin, the leading expert witness for the prosecution. They privately encouraged Servetus to believe that the case against him would be defeated, while some of them even supported him in public. For more than two months the proceedings dragged on, with Calvin frequently coming under attack from both the accused and those who were sitting in judgement. But the Libertines had chosen their ground badly. Despite his powerful presence and aggressive self-confidence, Servetus was a liability. His views were so extreme that they were eventually unsupportable, and when the Protestant Churches of Switzerland wrote to Geneva urging that the arch-heretic be burnt, his cause became hopeless. Even some of Calvin's enemies voted in favour of executing the prisoner. He was burned to death, the only heretic to suffer the death penalty in Calvin's Geneva. He died bravely, proclaiming his faith in a single God, whose son Jesus was born human but became part of God on his death. It was a distinction he was prepared to give his life to maintain.

Calvin's opponents abroad attacked him violently for the part he played in the Servetus affair. His critics in subsequent centuries have been equally censorious, while his supporters have made valiant efforts to exonerate him. The difficulty facing the historian is that it is not certain exactly what Calvin did do or, of course, what were the motives for his presumed actions. The pieces of evidence stressed by Calvin's supporters are that he had to be persuaded to allow Servetus to be denounced in Vienne, only agreeing with great reluctance; that he attempted to persuade the Genevan authorities to execute Servetus by beheading rather than by the more painful burning; and that he could have denounced Servetus many years earlier had he really wanted to destroy him. In contrast, his opponents make much of an extract from one of Calvin's letters of many years earlier in which he stated that if Servetus ever appeared in Geneva, he would not escape with his life. They also draw attention to the certainty that there was personal animosity between the two men, and the possibility that Calvin might have been acting out of vindictiveness. On balance, the affair does not reflect well on Calvin. It would, of course, be anachronistic to attack him for his intolerance – the supporters of religious toleration were few and far between in the mid-sixteenth century and were considered to be as extreme as Servetus in their own way – but his justification of the need to kill Servetus is not very convincing. It would have been more in keeping with the spirit of his teaching if this heretic had been expelled as were the others who had disagreed with him and lost. There can be little doubt that Calvin felt strongly about Servetus as a person, and there is good reason to believe that he deluded himself into thinking that his great animosity was motivated by a desire to protect the good name of God. His judgement seems to have been coloured to some extent by his feelings of hatred, and the best that can be said is that he at least showed that he was human!

The Servetus affair was equally important for the effect it had on the political situation in Geneva. It marked the turning point in the struggle for supremacy between Perrin, Calvin and their respective supporters. It is not clear why the decision to execute Servetus heralded such a definite shift in the balance of power, but from then onwards the Libertines were thrown onto the defensive and were gradually forced to yield ground on the key issues. Their eclipse was probably facilitated by the loss of public credibility that followed their espousal of the cause of a man whom Calvin successfully portrayed as a major threat to religious order, and was brought about by many of the 'waverers' concluding that Calvin's policies were preferable to the alternatives. The end did not come all at once, but the signs were clear. The long-running dispute over where the power to excommunicate lay was resolved in the Consistory's favour. The policy of excluding immigrants from citizenship was reversed, although membership of the elected Councils continued to be restricted to native-born Genevans; and the election of the Syndics for 1555 resulted in the Libertines' complete defeat and the transfer of the day-to-day control of events to Calvin's supporters. In May 1555, in what seems to have been a spontaneous attempt, while under the influence of drink, to stage a *coup* by stirring up an anti-immigrant riot, the leading Libertines placed themselves in an indefensible position. Following the failure of their ill-planned attempt to seize power, most of them had the good sense to recognise that their cause was hopeless, and to flee the city, carrying with them whatever they could. Those who remained were questioned under torture, tried and executed. Calvin's victory was to all intents and purposes complete.

3 The Years of Supremacy

Theodore Beza, Calvin's first biographer and his successor as leader of the Church in Geneva, was in no doubt of the significance of the defeat of the Libertines. He believed that 'the devil departed with the fugitives'. Certainly the change was dramatic. Calvin's influence was now paramount. His advice was sought and followed on almost all matters, even on the quality of the city's first dentist, and on the necessity of houses having railings around their balconies for the safety of children. Nor was he slow to point out where the law needed to be strengthened and punishments to be increased in order to discourage evildoers. Geneva rapidly became a city in which there was but one standard of behaviour, with those who failed to follow it being severely punished for their affrontery. Never had the members of such a large community – it was nearing 20,000 by 1560, thanks to the large influx of refugees – lived such highly supervised and disciplined lives, with seemingly every aspect of their existence being subject to close control.

To visitors, the most obvious signs of Calvin's influence were in matters of everyday behaviour. The people were soberly dressed with no unnecessary ornamentation. They spoke to each other courteously and with seeming concern for one another's interests. Public entertainments were non-existent, and singing was only to be heard in the churches, in which virtually the entire population assembled several times each week to praise God and to listen to sermons. Geneva's famous night-life, based on licensed prostitutes and rowdy taverns, had disappeared. John Knox, who subsequently brought Calvinism to Scotland, lived in the city at the time. He was not easily impressed, but felt compelled to write that Geneva

> is the most perfect school of Christ that ever was in the earth since the days of the Apostles. In other places, I confess Christ to be truly preached; but manners and religion to be so sincerely reformed, I have not yet seen in any other place.

It was possible to ensure these changes in behaviour because the Councils were now prepared to pass the necessary edicts and to back up the Consistory in enforcing them. At the same time, the Consistory was given a much freer hand in bringing wrong-doers to justice. No longer did it have to rely on the Little Council to act against challenges to its authority, for it was now granted the power to summon people, both the accused and the witnesses, to come before it and to answer whatever questions they were asked. The influence of the ministers had always been great in the Consistory, but they had not been able to rely on it being overwhelming. The fact that meetings were chaired by one of the Syndics, who carried his baton of office as a symbol of his authority, was a sign of their supposed subservience. It was therefore a move of considerable significance, and not merely a gesture, when it was agreed that the Syndic, who would still chair the meetings, would no longer carry his baton with him. The virtual autonomy of the Consistory, with its majority of ministers reflecting the growth of the Church since 1541, was recognised. And with the acceptance that the ministers would effectively exercise a veto in the selection of elders, the power of Calvin was further reinforced. His political 'system' was complete when the Little Council agreed to adopt the procedure of regular mutual self-criticism that had been Calvin's most powerful tool in winning control of the Venerable Company of Ministers in the years after 1541. Although this self-criticism was to be conducted in private, the fact that it was scrupulously carried out meant that no issue could be side-stepped – the technique that had regularly been used with success by his opponents.

   * Writers hostile to Calvin had traditionally criticised two aspects of his control of Geneva. They have highlighted the harsh punishments meted out to those who did not conform and they have bemoaned the loss of personal freedom that resulted from the detailed regulation of life in the city. Certainly it cannot be denied that, under Calvin's influence, the severity of sentence for some crimes increased considerably, and became more draconian than almost anywhere else in Europe. Especially noticeable was the higher price paid by the sexually promiscuous for their activities. One of the more public parts of Calvin's running battles with his opponents on the Little Council during the late 1540s and early 1550s had been his fury at the nominal punishments that adultery incurred. A few days in prison – barely an inconvenience for those who could afford to take their servants with them – was considered severe! Calvin was not content until it was agreed that persistent adulterers would face the death penalty, although it should be noted that as banishment preceded this, it was only those who were as foolhardy as Servetus who ran the risk of execution, the men by beheading and the women by drowning.

   That the punishments in Geneva became harsh and excessive, even for a violent age, is clearly proven. The number of executions rose considerably, reaching double figures per year when previously they had been a rarity, and there are numerous examples of individuals being treated in a way that has shocked later generations. Critics have taken particular delight in recounting the ways in which people convicted of speaking out against Calvin and his teachings were punished, one, for instance, by having his tongue pierced. But it would be incorrect to imagine that Geneva in any way approximated to a modern police state. It seems that, in general, only those who flaunted their 'unacceptable' behaviour were likely to be charged with a crime, and that it was very usual for those who appeared contrite and promised not to transgress again merely to be warned about their future conduct. The desire for retribution was normally less strong than the wish to encourage reformation.

* It was this determination to change people, even in the smallest detail of their daily lives, that has seemed particularly obnoxious to many nineteenth and twentieth century liberals. It was also the major cause of the large amount of opposition that Calvin faced within the city up to 1555. The justification put forward for this high level of interference will be explored in a later chapter (see page 44), but it is clear that it won little sympathy outside the city among established reformers, to whom it smacked of the excesses of some of the Anabaptist groups. That Calvin persevered with this unpopular approach for so many years in such an unpromising situation, and was eventually triumphant – even if partly due to events outside his control – tells us much about the man. It also illustrates the source of many of the hostile judgements that Calvin was in reality a petty-minded dictator who was unable to distinguish what was important from what was insignificant.

It is not to be wondered at that writers, including historians from the first half of the twentieth century, have delighted in highlighting examples of restrictions that readers are likely to find laughable or absurd. So attention has been drawn to the unsuccessful attempt to replace taverns with meeting places where sober conversation could take place amidst periodic readings from the Bible, or the steps taken to control the names given to children so that frivolous or irreverent ones could be avoided. Other puritanical regulations have been cited which give a more accurate impression of the atmosphere Calvin generated. The Consistory spent much time in stamping out what it regarded as being the four outstanding forms of profane behaviour – sex outside marriage, singing outside church, dancing at any time, and clothing that was unnecessarily decorative.

It seems likely that sexual morality in Geneva was more lax than in much of Europe. Calvin certainly thought so, and the recorded evidence contains many reflections, among both men and women, of the attitude that adultery was an acceptable and accepted social custom. It is, of course, impossible to offer quantitative evidence of any reduction in promiscuity as a result of Calvin's influence, but circumstantial evidence suggests that he was not highly successful. The fact that former prostitutes, once the licensing system lapsed, regularly returned to the city after being expelled implies that they still found a ready source of customers. Perhaps even more telling, and especially painful and embarrassing for Calvin, was the fact that at the height of his power and influence both his step-daughter and his sister-in-law were banished after admitting to adultery, one with Calvin's own servant. But perhaps the bitterest blow of all came in 1558 when Guillaume Farel, his closest friend and associate although since 1538 at a distance, announced that he was about to marry a girl young enough to be his grand-daughter. This came at a time when Calvin had at last been successful in outlawing the custom whereby older men who lost their wives normally married girls in their teens, and he felt outraged that his friend should so let him down. Forgiveness only came with the approach of death.

It was easier to deal with singing, dancing and dressing for show, as these were normally done at least semi-publicly. The pace of change was slow while the opposition was strong, especially as much of Perrin's bitterness towards Calvin was caused by the vendetta that the reformer seemed to be waging against Perrin's relations for dancing at family celebrations. Calvin gained little sympathy from this campaign, or from his attempts to prevent gentlewomen from marking their social position by adorning themselves in silk or with fancy lace accoutrements. But when Perrin began to equip the city's militia, for which he was responsible as Captain-General, in showy uniforms merely to offend Calvin, public sentiment swung round to support increased restrictions. Once again, the opposition had overplayed its hand and had squandered a strong position. It is not surprising that after the Libertines were expelled, Geneva quickly became the city of sober dress and behaviour of which commentators such as Knox so strongly approved.

4 Education

Besides Calvin's increased power and the use he made of it to continue the process of building Geneva into the City of God, the years of his ascendancy were marked by the achievement of a specific goal he had set himself from the outset. As the *Ecclesiastical Ordinances* of 1541 had shown, Calvin understood the importance of establishing a high quality centre of learning that would be able to train the future generation of leaders for both Church and state. But his efforts in this direction had largely been frustrated by a shortage of funds and by the unavailability of suitably expert teachers. The destruction of the opposition meant that it became possible to make the foundation of an Academy a high priority in the use of the city's very limited financial resources. At the same time good fortune once again smiled on Calvin in that the famous teachers of neighbouring Lausanne fell out with the authorities of Berne, who controlled the town, and were prepared to move to Geneva *en masse*.

So, in 1559, the Academy was officially opened, although as was normal in such matters, the buildings were not completed for a number of years to come. It fulfilled the roles of both a school and a university, and rapidly established for itself a reputation as an educational centre of excellence. When he had first formulated his ideas on the importance of education, Calvin had in mind the needs of the local community. But by the time the Academy became a reality, Calvin and Geneva had become the focus of attention for reformers from much of Europe, and the Academy attracted hundreds of students from abroad within a few years of its opening. These students, of course, became the effective missionaries of Calvinism, and they went forth in much greater numbers than had been possible in earlier years, when only the few had been able to gather around Calvin on an individual basis to learn from him directly. In some ways Calvin viewed the Academy as the most pleasing of his achievements.

This is not surprising as Calvin always stressed the importance of education. Historians have tended to concentrate on the unusual or dramatic features of his life – his skill as an organiser, his emphasis on discipline, his struggles with his opponents and his belief in predestination – and have generally underrated the importance of some of his more mundane activities. Parker, in his biography of Calvin, made strenuous efforts to redress the balance, and argued convincingly that the really important changes in Geneva were brought about as a result of the people's long exposure to the reformer's preaching. It can be seen that the political defeat of the Libertines was important, but it would have counted for little had there not existed the large body of the population who had already been convinced of the correctness of his teachings. It was particularly significant that a generation had grown up from childhood to responsible adulthood having been carefully instructed in his beliefs. He was a tireless and systematic preacher, guiding his congregation through the Bible line by line in a sequence of sermons that ran into thousands. He also taught his fellow-preachers as far as was necessary to ensure that the people were consistently instructed in the correct understanding of God's words, and disagreements were discussed until his colleagues accepted his interpretation or, in some cases, were forced to leave the city. The fact that the population as a whole was more knowledgeable about the Bible than any other large group of people had ever been marked out the Geneva of Calvin's period of supremacy as particularly noteworthy.

5 Was Geneva a Theocracy?

It has frequently been claimed that in his final years Calvin turned Geneva into a theocracy. This means that the city was ruled by the religious leaders whose aim was the creation of a society that was guided in all matters by the word of God. It has mainly been Calvin's critics who have stressed this issue, and in doing so they have tended to imply that he in some way over-stepped the mark by assuming powers that rightly lay with others. Certainly, if their factual claims are valid, they have been making a significant point, because they have been drawing attention to a feature that marked out Geneva as different from every other reformed state of the time. Whereas the norm was for the secular power, whether a prince or a city council, to remain firmly in control of the major decision-making processes, they have maintained that in Geneva this passed to Calvin and his fellows of the Venerable Company of Ministers. Some commentators have taken the point further and have stated that Calvin became, in effect, a dictator.

Writers sympathetic to Calvin have generally attempted to modify this interpretation. Their approach has been to attack it on two fronts. They have challenged the contention that the Church assumed direct political control in Geneva, mainly by drawing attention to the fact that there were no changes in the constitutional arrangements for the government of the city whereby this could have happened. They have argued that for a state to be a theocracy the Church must be in control of the major organs of government, and that in Geneva this was not the case. They have also made much of Calvin's denials that he had any political ambitions. They have stressed that he made no effort to become a citizen until pressed to do so in 1559, largely in order to prove that he aspired to no position of civil authority, and that neither he nor any of the other ministers were members of any of the councils. They have shown that Calvin took active steps to discourage the cult of personality, even going to the lengths of insisting that when he died his body should be buried in an unmarked grave, as in fact it was.

It is interesting to note that the historians who have discussed this issue have generally revealed an underlying assumption that theocracy is wrong. They have tended either to accuse Calvin of a crime or to defend him against what they consider to be unfounded charges. Rarely has there been even a hint that it might be a good thing for religious leaders to be in power. Perhaps this is an indication of how ingrained in western society is the concept of the secular state, a situation that has made it very difficult for us to understand twentieth century phenomena such as the Iranian revolution. However, to reach a valid assessment of Calvin's work in Geneva it is necessary to abandon such assumptions and to concentrate our attention on what was done, for what motives and with what effects. On this basis it is possible to conclude that the 'theocracy' debate has suffered by being viewed from a hostile stance. In the light of the available evidence it appears to be most helpful to conclude that during his years of ascendancy Calvin was able to exert massive influence on the government of his state without there ever being a formal arrangement to reflect the true nature of the situation, and that he used his influence to ensure that the entire population came as close as possible to living the type of life that the Bible indicated was God's wish for mankind. In the process he effectively wielded the power that we associate with a dictator, although he studiously avoided becoming embroiled in the associated trappings of pomp and affluence. If he had lived in a medieval kingdom he would

bouring country. An unjust hatred for the House of Savoy attracted to
their standard a large body of patriots, who, aspiring after a democratic

I. CALVIN

Fig. 323.—John Calvin, called the Pope of Geneva, chief of the so-called Reformed Church ;
born at Noyon in 1509, died at Geneva in 1564.—Fac-simile of a Wood Engraving from the
works of Theodore Beza, translated from the Latin by Simon Goulart—" Les Vrais Pour-
traits des Hommes Illustres " (4to, Jean de Laon, Geneva, 1581).—One of the engraved
frontispieces of this collection bears the monogram of Jean Cousin.

Page from a nineteenth century book on Heresies

have been described as being the power behind the throne: as it was, he
became the irresistible mentor of the many individuals who collectively
made up the government of his adopted city.

Yet important as Calvin was in the history of Geneva, it was as an international figure that he achieved his greatest historical significance. The happenings within the city state illuminate his aims and his methods, and provided a working example for others to follow, but without an understanding of his teachings and of the assumptions that lay behind them it is impossible to arrive at an appreciation of his importance, either during his own lifetime or in the centuries that followed. The next chapter explores his basic assumptions and the teachings that flowed from them.

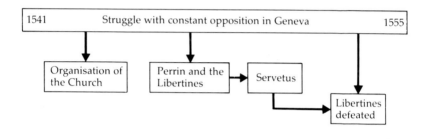

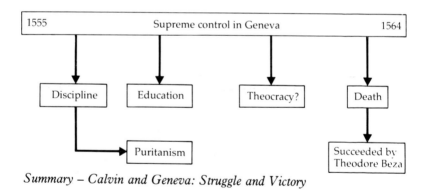

Summary – Calvin and Geneva: Struggle and Victory

Making notes on 'Calvin and Geneva: Struggle and Victory'

Make three sections of notes from this chapter. The first two sections can be made directly from the text. These are on 'The opposition to Calvin' and 'The use Calvin made of his victory'. The third section will need more thought. Under the heading 'Calvin the man', make a list of characteristics that help to describe him as a person. Next to each characteristic, note down your evidence for this. You may find it helpful to divide your list into 'Strengths' and 'Weaknesses'.

The following headings, subheadings and questions may help your note-making:

1.   Struggles with the opposition
1.1. The nature of the opposition. Why was Calvin opposed?
1.2. Ami Perrin and the Libertines
2.   Michael Servetus. Why was the Servetus affair so important?
3.   The years of supremacy
3.1. Calvin's increased power
3.2. Punishments
3.3. Changes in behaviour
4.   Education. What was the significance of the Academy?
5.   Theocracy. Was Geneva a theocracy in Calvin's later years?

Answering essay questions on 'Calvin and Geneva'
The greatest likelihood is that you will need to use evidence from this
and the previous chapter in answering a general question about Calvin
and Calvinism – and not in writing specifically about his life or his work
in Geneva. But it is possible that, at some stage, you will be expected to
construct a whole essay from the material you have just read. In such an
essay you are almost certain to be required to present an analysis rather
than a narrative, by being faced with a question that asks 'Why?' or
'How far?' rather than 'What?' Examples might be:

1. 'Why was Calvin unable to impose his will on the people of
    Geneva until after 1555?'
2. 'Why were Calvin's opponents in Geneva successful for so long?'
3. 'How far was Calvin successful in putting his ideas into practice
    in Geneva?'
4. 'How far did Calvin create a new society as well as a new Church
    in Geneva?'

You should be careful not to be lured into writing long narrative
passages that are not directly linked to the wording of the question. The
temptation will be particularly strong with questions like the first one,
where it is possible to construct an essay around one answer such as
'because of the strength of the opposition he faced'. But never let
yourself select a 'Why?' question where you can think of only one
'because' answer. You should always be able to think of at least three,
and preferably four or five. If you cannot, you do not know enough to
tackle the question successfully. Make a list of as many 'because'
answers as possible to questions 1 and 2.

'How far?' questions are normally answered by two-part essays. The
first part concentrates on explaining 'To this extent YES', while in the
second part you explain 'To this extent NO'. But there is sometimes the
need to add a third section. This is particularly so when the question
makes an assumption that requires justification or includes a concept
that needs explanation. In the examples given above, question 4 makes

an assumption, and question 3 needs an explanation. What are they? At what point in your essay would you include them?

Source-based questions on '*Calvin and Geneva: Struggle and Victory*'

1 The state of religion in Geneva, 1536 and 1559
Read carefully the descriptions of the state of religion in Geneva in 1536 (on page 12) and in 1559 (on page 29). Answer the following questions:
a) What is meant by 'reformation' in the first extract?
b) What is meant by 'manners' in the second extract?
c) What contribution does the phrase 'it is true' make to the tone of the first extract, and the phrase 'I confess' to the tone of the second extract?
d) The authors of the two extracts shared a similar perception of the changes that had taken place in Geneva between 1536 and 1559. What was this perception? Support your answer with evidence from the extracts.
e) What was the historical significance of the changes that took place in Geneva between 1536 and 1559?

2 Portraits of Calvin
Study carefully the three portraits of Calvin reproduced on pages 16, 35, and 90. Answer the following questions:
a) Which of the portraits is likely to be least inaccurate? Justify your answer.
b) Present as much evidence as possible to suggest that the illustration reproduced on page 35 was probably selected by the author of the book on heresies in order to portray Calvin in a poor light.
c) What is the likely dating of the portraits reproduced on pages 16 and 90? Justify your answers.
d) What techniques are used by the artist of the wood engraving reproduced on page 90 to communicate approval of Calvin?
e) What are the limitations of these portraits as evidence of Calvin's personality and character? Is the same true of all portraits of historical figures?

CHAPTER 4

Calvin's Religious Thinking

1 Introduction

Calvin has traditionally been presented as the Reformation leader who brought order and coherence to the disorganised and fragmented theologies that had emerged during the first phase of the reform movement. He has been described as the sound and efficient codifier of other men's thinking, who fulfilled a most useful function in arranging, simplifying and popularising the previously chaotic collection of Protestant teachings. This is a generally sound and perceptive interpretation of Calvin the theologian, but it has a weakness in that it implies that his religious thinking lacked any real spark of originality. He has therefore been viewed as the 'artisan' rather than the 'artist'; as the borrower of others' ideas rather than the generator of his own. A number of historians have even been prepared to devote the major part of their working lives to tracking down the sources of his ideas. They have done this by combing through his writings alongside those works of other theologians that were available to him, and spotting similarities. They have been given increased scope for their researches by the fact that Calvin frequently revised his major theological work, *Christianae Religionis Institutio*, publishing new editions in both Latin and French almost up to the time of his death. So with the Latin editions of 1536, 1539, 1543, 1550 and 1559, and the French editions of 1541, 1545, 1551 and 1560 as evidence, there has been plenty of opportunity to piece together the way in which his ideas changed and developed in the light of his experiences and further study. The result has been varying claims that Calvin was mainly influenced by Saint Augustine, by the medieval theologian Duns Scotus, by Martin Luther and by Martin Bucer, his great friend and mentor during his exile in Strasbourg, while gaining nothing at all from Ulrich Zwingli, whom he clearly regarded as being second-rate.

Convincing as these arguments seem, and illuminating as they are of the genesis of his thinking, they do appear to deflect our attention from what is historically significant about Calvin the theologian. It is no doubt interesting to establish as far as possible the stages by which a thinker came to take up the position he did, but it is of much greater importance to establish what he actually taught and to estimate the effects of his teachings on others. Calvin's claim to be one of the foremost leaders of the Reformation rests largely on the fact that his writings were used to mould the thoughts and actions of hundreds of thousands of his fellow believers both during his lifetime and in the centuries that followed. This will not be changed whatever conclusions we reach about the extent to which his ideas were unique.

Equally, it could be argued that the large amount of historians' time that has been devoted to researching the origins of Calvin's thinking has led to a clear underestimation of the relative extent of his originality. It is very rare for any thinker to have a totally new thought. Much more frequently, originality is demonstrated by joining together existing thoughts in new combinations and presenting them in a way that gives them an enhanced meaning. Calvin certainly did a large amount of this. The concentration on tracking down the origin of individual elements of his thinking has masked such aspects of his creativity. It seems likely that if there were sufficient evidence about the development of other theologians' thinking, it would not be possible to establish a clear distinction between them on the one hand and Calvin on the other hand, in terms of creativity or, possibly, originality. Certainly, it has already been established that Martin Luther, for example, drew many of his individual ideas from the writings of earlier theologians, although there has been no suggestion that he lacked originality. The debate on the extent of Calvin's contribution to new thinking is perhaps best described as an interesting backwater of historical study, which has been explored in a rather negative and unfair way, with the presumed intention of diminishing Calvin's intellectual stature. It deserves to be known, but is likely to be of only passing interest to all but students of the history of theology. This chapter will therefore concentrate on those aspects of Calvin's contribution to the theology of the Reformation which had a widespread effect.

   * In reaching conclusions about what Calvin taught and the effects of his teachings, a conscious effort must be made to distinguish between what he meant and what he was thought to have meant. Both, of course, had a significant effect on his own and later times, because it is the message that is received – rather than the one that is given out – that affects people, but it should be remembered that only one is relevant when making judgements about the soundness of the teaching. This task is not an easy one, for not only did his enemies, especially Catholic writers, publish purposely perverted accounts of his teachings, but his supporters also re-interpreted his work, giving aspects of it new emphases. It is, in fact, because of the efforts of his followers that the balance of Calvin's teachings is still widely misunderstood. For instance, it has been the generally received wisdom since the mid-nineteenth century that the core of Calvin's theology is his teaching on predestination (see page 45). This misunderstanding, which has been highlighted by recent research, came about because leading Calvinists taught that this was so. Yet it now seems that Calvin never intended this to happen.

   Equally widespread is the misapprehension that Calvin largely ignored Jesus and the New Testament and concentrated instead on God the Father and the Old Testament – an understandable misinterpretation, and one that has been common since the sixteenth century, because Calvin unintentionally encouraged it within his own writings. He differed from other reformers, such as Martin Luther and Ulrich Zwingli, by according equal status to all parts of the Bible. Whereas most Reformation theologians regarded the Old Testament as significant mainly because of the light it shed on the New Testament, Calvin viewed it as a vital part of God's revelation of himself to mankind, as well as illuminating many aspects of the life of Jesus in Palestine. As a result he laid himself open to the charge that he failed to give sufficient prominence in his teaching to the traditional view of the Trinity, in which God the Father, God the Son and God the Holy Spirit were seen to be mysteriously separate yet unified, and of equal importance one to the other. He seemed to be concentrating on one-third of the Trinity. A large part of the strong antipathy felt towards him by the Zwinglian Church of Berne was on account of this. As early as the 1540s he was having to defend himself in public debate against the charge that he was in reality a unitarian, downgrading Jesus and the Holy Spirit to a status inferior to that of God the Father. His defence can now be seen to be convincing, but it is not to be wondered at that, as Calvinism developed and spread, the dread of God seemed to be much more thought and taught about than was the love of Jesus. So it must be remembered that Calvin's religious thinking and the teachings of institutionalised Calvinism should not be taken as being synonymous.

 * Our major source of information about what Calvin actually taught is undoubtedly his *Christianae Religionis Institutio*, although much can also be learnt from his huge output of commentaries on individual books of the Bible, from the surviving transcripts of many of his sermons, and from many of his letters to fellow theologians, in which he discussed some of the finer points of his thinking. There is good reason to suppose that the *Institutio* was an accurate record of Calvin's intended teaching. He appears to have been at pains – often literally, as much of his work was done while suffering agonies of discomfort from internal ailments – to ensure that each new edition was as clear a statement of his thinking as it was possible for him to make. This involved him in considerable restructuring of the book as it grew from a slim volume that could be slipped into the pocket into a mighty tome with hundreds of additional pages. Such an expansion was the result of Calvin's determination to clarify any aspect of his thinking which was attacked as being obscure, as well as to state his position on whatever theological issues were causing major controversy at the time of each revision.

Further confidence is gained in the reliability of the *Institutio* as an accurate reflection of Calvin's thinking by the purposes that lay behind the book's production. Part of its lengthy sub-title was 'The basic teaching of the Christian religion comprising almost the whole sum of godliness and whatever it is necessary to know on the doctrine of salvation', suggesting that the intention was to provide ordinary Christians with a clear statement of what they should believe. Calvin never lost sight of this aim to provide an accessible overview of basic Christian theology, even in the later editions when he was primarily aiming his remarks at the serious student who was training for the ministry. In these circumstances he took great care to spell out exactly what he meant, although, of course, there has subsequently been considerable disagreement among historians about the interpretation of a number of his statements. Unfortunately the situation has been somewhat confused by the fact that the preparation of the French editions, which were designed as no more than straight translations of the most recent Latin version, was probably largely delegated to assistants whose work was full of minor errors, and partly undertaken by Calvin himself in a great hurry and with resulting errors. The outcome of this has been to present historians with sufficient raw material for doubts to be generated about the exact stance Calvin took on some matters of detail. But this in no way discredits the argument that in all essentials the *Institutio* fairly reflects his developing thinking, and that the Latin edition of 1559 is a reliable source of his final position.

2 Assumptions

All thinking people carry around with them sets of assumptions. Mostly, these have never been consciously chosen nor even recognised. In an extreme form, an assumption can become a prejudice. In a modern liberal society, it is generally accepted that all assumptions are challengeable and that the reasonable person is prepared to change his assumptions if he is unable to justify them. Nowadays there are few assumptions that are in practice universally held: diversity is the norm, especially between parents and their nearly-adult children. But in previous centuries – and certainly in sixteenth century Europe – the opposite was the case. It was widely accepted that without commonly accepted assumptions, especially about what was right and what was important, society would disintegrate and chaos would reign. To be different was dangerous and often resulted in death – as the tens of thousands of people accused of witchcraft found to their cost. The Reformation was so savagely repressed in many quarters partly because its leaders challenged so many of the assumptions of the time.

In a number of respects Calvin was a very typical Protestant. He shared with Luther, Zwingli, Melanchthon, Bucer and the other famed publicists a set of assumptions that generally marked out the reformers as being different from the Catholics. First and foremost he was an evangelical, believing in the Bible as the most complete revelation of God and His purposes that was available to humanity. It was this dedication to the Bible as the word of God that marked out the Protestants, whether Lutheran, Zwinglian or Calvinist, from the Catholics and the radicals, generally known as Anabaptists, who assumed that knowledge of God came, to a significant extent, from other sources. Yet, despite their preaching of the dogma of *sola Scriptura* (only accepting teachings that sprang from the text of the Bible), neither Calvin nor the other leading Protestant theologians were what today would be called fundamentalists or literalists. They did not believe that God's message had been laid out in simple terms for all who looked to see. They rationalised the seeming contradictions within the Scriptures by assuming that God's intervention, through the agency of the Holy Spirit, was necessary for the correct meaning to be recognised. Thus they assumed that if the Bible was not read through the eyes of faith, erroneous interpretations would result. By exercising the somewhat twisted logic that was common to all those blessed with religious certainty, Calvin came to believe that the test of true faith was that a person should agree with his interpretation of the Bible in every detail. And, of course, given the other assumptions that he had made about the nature of the Bible and the part played by the Holy Spirit in revealing its single meaning, he had no alternative to believing as he did.

Yet, while agreeing with the evangelical assumptions of mainstream Protestantism, Calvin stood out as differing in detail from the other leading theologians. He could be described as being more hard-line, extreme or doctrinaire over the Bible. Many were prepared to accept that the Bible was made up of books of varying status, and that God's revelation was more complete in some than in others. A few were even prepared to face the possibility that portions of the Bible had been incorrectly included as a result of human error. But to Calvin such a suggestion was blasphemy of the highest order. He showed the severity of his view when one of his colleagues in Geneva was unwise enough to suggest that the Song of Solomon, part of the Old Testament and now widely regarded as being an erotic poem with spiritual overtones, should be excluded from the Scriptures. The 'culprit' was hounded from the city and efforts were made to ensure that he would not be welcomed elsewhere. This had to happen if Calvin was to defend his assumption that the entire Bible was God's one, and complete, way of communicating with humanity. He made further public witness of his view of the Bible both by devoting a large proportion of his time to the preparation of commentaries to aid believers in the understanding of the Scriptures, and by basing every part of his teaching explicitly on texts from either the Old or New Testaments.

* Calvin's other basic theological assumptions were about the nature of God, the nature of Man and the relationship between them. In common with most theologians, irrespective of the religion they followed, he took it for granted that God was all-powerful, all-knowing and was the Creator of the Universe. He also fully accepted the assumptions that God was just – which had been passed on from Judaism to Christianity – and that He intervened directly in daily life on earth, which was an integral part of the Christian tradition.

1 Suppose a man falls among thieves, or wild beasts; is shipwrecked
at sea by a sudden gale; is killed by a falling house or tree.
Suppose another man wandering through the desert finds help in
his straits; having been tossed by the waves reaches harbour;
5 miraculously escapes death by a finger's breadth. Carnal reason
ascribes all such happenings, whether favourable or adverse, to
fortune. But anyone who has been taught by Christ's lips that all
the hairs of his head are numbered will look farther afield for a
cause, and will deem that all events are governed by God's secret
10 counsels.

But, in contrast to Luther and many of the other leading reformers,
he did not assume that God was loving. It was this omission that has led
many commentators to stigmatise him as being cold, uncaring and
severe in his teachings. It has also given rise to the suggestion that he
was more interested in the God of the Old Testament, who was full of
wrath and retribution, than in the God of the New Testament, who was
portrayed by Jesus as caring for the whole of His creation. Most such
judgements have been intended by their authors to be criticisms of
Calvin, who was clearly out of step with the generally accepted
assumptions about the nature of God that were current when the
comments were made. Such a view is now shared by most students of
Calvin, whatever their religious affiliation (if any), because they belong
to western, secular, liberal-democratic societies which assume that the
ideal relationship is one based on mutual love and affection. For Calvin
to assume that God does not share this view is to make him, for most of
us, a character with whom we find it difficult to sympathise. But given
the life experiences of sixteenth century European man, in which
physical and emotional violence were much more common than love or
caring, and in which daily misery and sudden death were widely shared
expectations, it is little wonder that Calvin assumed as he did, or that
many were prepared to accept his assumption without question. To do
otherwise was likely to have been the result of wishful thinking. What
was happening all around the known world seemed clearly to indicate
that if God was responsible for what took place in his creation, he was
much more interested in justice than in loving. It also appeared to
justify Calvin's basic assumptions about the nature of Man.
    ★ Calvin assumed that Man is both insignificant and evil. He thought
about the whole of the universe and the whole of time and concluded
that, in comparison with them, an individual human being is as
nothing. He contemplated his own thoughts and actions and recognised
that he fell short of his ideal in all respects. At the same time he saw that
he was virtuous compared with most people – a thought that confirmed
him in his assumption about the sinfulness of Man. How could it be
otherwise if God chose to afflict the world with so many tribulations, for
God was just and would not punish the innocent? His assumptions

about the nature and importance of Man were at the heart of many of his decisions, and so he was genuinely careless with his own and others' lives and comfort, believing that what happened to the individual was of no real consequence. Assuming, as he did, that God was in control of everything, he needed to give no thought to the consequences of his actions. He merely needed to ensure that, at any moment, he was acting as God directed.

* Herein lay assumptions about the relationship between God and Man, and the purpose of life. Calvin was filled with awe at the distance between the greatness of God and the insignificance of Man. He could envisage no relationship between them other than that between master and slave. It was for God to command and for Man to obey. God was therefore only approachable on terms of abject self-effacement, for he could not possibly be interested in the needs or desires of an individual human being. Man's whole existence should be directed to meeting God's wishes, not his own. This, in fact, was what Calvin assumed was the purpose of life, for he could see no other and could not accept that life might be purposeless. Given that God was great beyond all imagining, and that He had created the universe and all that was in it, He must have had some reason for doing so, and especially for creating Man. Calvin had to assume that the purpose of all life was to glorify God. It followed that any action which was not motivated by a desire to carry out that purpose was wicked and should if possible be prevented. At the very least it would be punished.

Yet, despite all his certainty, Calvin always worked from an assumption of limited knowledge. One way in which he described the relationship between God and Man was as between the knowing and the unknowing. Therefore he was not in the least abashed at frequently admitting in his teachings that there were gaps in his understanding and seemingly unresolvable contradictions in his beliefs. When challenged, he was always able to answer that he was merely explaining God's message as it was given, and that everybody must accept that more remained hidden than was revealed. With literal meaning and all sincerity, he could frequently maintain that 'only God knows'.

3 Predestination

The most widely known aspect of Calvin's religious thinking is that about predestination. In many ways his ideas flowed naturally from the assumptions he had made about the nature of God and His relationship to Man. If God was all-knowing, it followed that He must have always known everything that was going to happen throughout the whole universe. And if He was all-powerful, it must be that nothing could happen unless He willed it. So it was impossible to avoid the conclusion that every action of every person was not only pre-known by God, but, because He had actively willed them, they were pre-destined by Him.

Numerous implications stemmed from this simple doctrine. Most significant were those that had to do with salvation. Luther had started his agitation against the teachings of the Church because he disagreed with the current doctrine on the subject (see *Luther and the German Reformation* in this series). He objected to the belief that salvation was to be earned by merit, each Christian needing to build up enough 'credit' points to outweigh the de-merits that had been amassed by the committing of sins. He wished to replace this doctrine with the belief that salvation was a freely given gift from God, available to all who would have faith in Him and His Son, Jesus Christ. He taught that salvation was the result of 'faith alone' (*sola fide*). In the process, of course, although he differed dramatically with the teaching of the Catholic Church, he was at one with them in accepting that salvation did not come automatically. The person wishing for salvation had to do something to acquire it.

Calvin was so convinced of the wretchedness and insignificance of Man in comparison to God that he could not accept that any human action could possibly affect the outcome of God's judgement in any way. He therefore found Luther's teaching, dependent as it was on the individual's active acceptance of God's gift, totally unacceptable. He insisted that Man was powerless to influence his eternal fate, that the decision had been made by God at the beginning of time, and that it was unalterable. A person was either a member of the elect – the group that God had chosen to save – or a reprobate – one whom God had decided to damn. There was no choice but to accept God's decision whatever it might be. Luckily for the mental health of mankind, Calvin taught that it was impossible to tell who had been saved and who had been damned. This would only be known after death.

Yet it would be very misleading to suggest that Calvin was teaching any type of fatalism. He did all he could to discourage any idea that one should merely sit back and await the outcome of God's predetermination. He advocated that all should seek for God's grace by living a life that was pleasing to Him and, while admitting that good deeds could do nothing to earn that grace, he did accept that the ability to live a good life was a fairly sure indication that one was numbered among the elect. As the persecution of Protestants, especially in France and the Netherlands, intensified during the later years of his life he was also prepared to agree that those who were called upon to suffer for their faith were probably thereby receiving a sign of their election. He constantly encouraged the saints (those who considered themselves to be among the elect) to strive to achieve clearer and clearer signs of their election. Equally, he was not prepared to accept that the reprobate should be allowed to enjoy the fruits of their sins in peace as if they were individually blameless for their rejection by God. He was quick to suggest that those who considered themselves damned should not use this as an excuse to continue in their evil ways.

1 The reprobate wish to be considered excused in their sin on the grounds that they cannot avoid the necessity of sinning, especially since this sort of necessity is cast upon them by God's ordaining. But we deny that they are thus excused, because the ordinance of
5 God, by which they complain that they are destined to destruction, has its own equity – unknown, indeed, to us, but very sure. From this we conclude that the ills they bear are all inflicted upon them by God's most righteous judgement. Accordingly, we teach that they act perversely who seek out the source of their
10 condemnation, turn their eyes to the hidden sanctuary of God's plan and wink at the corruption of nature from which it really springs.

* Ever since the early middle ages, Christian theologians had been much concerned with the concept of free will. Their problem had been to resolve the seeming contradiction between the existence of an all-powerful and all-knowing God and the teaching that Man was free either to choose or to reject Him. By the late middle ages the views of those who upheld the cause of free will had prevailed, and it was generally believed that God had decided to test out each member of His special creation, the human race, by granting them the power to act as they freely decided. It was taught that by denying Himself the ability to control the decisions people made, except when they asked Him to, God had made it possible for individuals to assume responsibility for their own actions, and therefore to be in a position to be fairly judged for the lives they had lived. Sin and virtue could have real meaning and could justly be followed by eternal damnation in hell or eternal glory in heaven as appropriate. Those who had denied the existence of free will – and there had been many of them through the centuries – were treated as heretics by the Church and were burned unless they were prepared to recant (publicly state that their beliefs were wrong).

It is not surprising that when Calvin's thinking on predestination became widely known, he was thought to be agreeing with the earlier heretics who had denied the existence of free will. But he strenuously denied this charge and maintained throughout his life that his teachings were not incompatible with a belief in an element of free will. His subtle and complex arguments, which depended on the careful definition of terms and on fine shades of meaning, was understood by few and accepted by fewer. His followers were generally content to accept the popular view that their Church was effectively denying the existence of free will, and that in this they differed markedly from other Protestants. That is not to say that predestination was a uniquely Calvinist doctrine. All the main Protestant Churches accepted it as a minor element of their teaching, and Luther certainly believed in it. But not as Calvin did. The distinction was between single and double predestination. Other Protestants were quite prepared to accept the doctrine of single predestination – that God, being all-knowing, was already aware of the decisions that individuals would make throughout their lives, and therefore was able to predict whether they would be damned or saved. But they could not accept the idea of double predestination with its claim that God not only knew from the beginning of time which people He would save, but had also made a positive decision about who He would damn. To many Christians, the thought that God might have rejected them before they were born was inconceivable.

The implications of the doctrine of double predestination for beliefs about the nature of God caused great hostility to Calvin. Many people were horrified, and even scandalised, that a Church leader could teach that God not only created evil but that He would then punish people for decisions that He had made on their behalf. This seemed contrary to the nature of the God as revealed in much of the New Testament. But Calvin was unrepentant. He continued to teach in later editions of the *Institutio* that Man was as nothing compared to God, and that it was not for mere mortals to question the motives or intentions of the Almighty.

1 The decree, I admit, is a fearful one; and yet it is impossible to deny that God foreknew what the end of man was to be before He created him, because He had so ordained by His decree. If anyone inveighs at this point against the foreknowledge of God, he does 5 so rashly and thoughtlessly. Why indeed should the heavenly judge be blamed because He was not ignorant of what was to happen? . . . It ought not indeed to seem ridiculous for me to say that God not only foresaw the fall of the first man and in him the ruin of his posterity, but also brought it about in accordance with 10 His own will. For as it belongs to His wisdom to know beforehand everything that is to happen, so it belongs to His power to rule and direct everything by His hand.

And

1 The first man fell because God had judged that to be expedient. But of why He so judged we know nothing. Yet it is nevertheless certain that He would not have done so had He not seen that this would redound to the glory of His Name. But when mention is 5 made of the glory of God, let us think also of His righteousness, for that which deserves praise must necessarily be equitable. Man stumbles, then, even as God ordained that he should, but he stumbles on account of his depravity.

Nor could he really understand why there was so much controversy about what was only a minor part of his teaching. To him, predestination was just a natural consequence of simple truths about the nature of God, and was in no way central to his pattern of beliefs.

Some historians who are in sympathy with Calvin have echoed surprise at the way in which other commentators have made too much of predestination and have got it out of proportion. But they have failed to see that the historical significance of a view is often dependent on the way it is perceived by others and not on the importance ascribed to it by its originator. The doctrine of double predestination certainly played a major part in shaping the attitudes of many non-Calvanists towards this branch of Protestantism.

Whatever opinion one forms about the relative importance of the doctrine of predestination within the totality of Calvin's religious thinking, it must be recognised that it greatly affected the whole balance of his teaching. For Catholics, Lutherans and the smaller mainstream Protestant groups such as the Zwinglians, the core of their beliefs and teachings was salvation and the ways in which it might be gained. For Calvinists, it was a much less important issue, because there was little point in dwelling on a matter that was already decided and about which nothing could be known for certain until after death. Instead of devoting the major part of his attention to the question of salvation, Calvin centred his thinking on the natures of God and Man and the relationship between them. This he made very clear in the opening words of the *Institutio*:

> The entire sum of our wisdom, of that which deserves to be called true and certain wisdom, may be said to consist of two parts; namely, the knowledge of God, and of ourselves.

It was this emphasis which gave Calvinism much of its distinctive flavour.

4 The place of Jesus Christ

Some critics of Calvin's teaching have suggested that, with his heavy concentration on God the Father, he hardly qualifies as a Christian theologian. It has even been hinted that he experienced difficulty in finding a significant place for Christ within his theology. Such claims are undoubtedly inaccurate and unfair, and seem to have originated in writings that were patently anti-Calvin propaganda. But, as with all effective propaganda, there was sufficient truth in it for those who were already predisposed to think the worst of the reformer to believe it. Certainly the 'feel' of his teachings was that God the Father was of by far the greatest importance, even if a detailed analysis of what he actually wrote yields evidence to support a contrary view. It was this 'feel' that organised Calvinism tended to project in the following centuries.

So strong was this generalised perception of Calvin's religious thinking that numbers of French historians, especially in the years after the Second World War, felt the need to redress the balance. They presented what they considered to be a convincing case to support the contention that, not only was the widely held view misconceived, but that Jesus was actually central to Calvin's thinking. They undoubtedly overstated their case, as is now generally recognised, but they did useful work in proving that it was nonsensical to doubt the depth and sincerity of Calvin's Christian commitment. They clearly established that Jesus played an important and integral part in his theology, even if the argument that it was a central part has failed to convince most neutral observers.

It is, of course, quite understandable that the opinion should emerge that Calvin's theology did not really need Christ. A brief survey of his teaching could be made coherent without there being any mention of Jesus, especially if the emphases were to be those that Calvin himself proclaimed – the nature of God and the nature of Man. But it would be impossible to proceed far with any explanation of Calvin's view of the relationship between God and Man without introducing the Son of God into the discussion. Nor would his place be peripheral, for without him Calvin would have been left with the incongruity of a God who is meant to be just and equitable deciding to elect individuals who were sinful and unworthy (as all mankind was by Calvin's definition) to eternal bliss in heaven, which could in no way be seen as fair. Jesus had to be the answer. Calvin taught that it was because Jesus had taken onto himself all the sins of mankind, and had died on the cross as a result, that the elect were justified (made worthy) in the eyes of God. Without that supreme sacrifice, there could be no salvation, for Man was totally unable to justify himself by his own efforts.

Yet in solving one problem in this way, Calvin was automatically creating many more, a situation faced by all Christian theologians. It was a fundamental tenet of all Christians that Jesus, as part of the Trinity, was divine. As such, he must therefore be perfect. How was it, then, that a just God could condemn His divine Son to die for the sins of others? Calvin's answer was sometimes to fall back on the logically sound but emotionally unsatisfying argument that if God was just He could do nothing unjust, and therefore the punishment of Jesus must be just, even if mere mortals could not understand how this was so. At other times he attempted to provide a more satisfying answer by distinguishing between the divine nature of Jesus, as the Son of God, and his human nature as a member of mankind. By this device, he was able to argue that it had been Jesus the man who had been punished, which of course was just because he had inherited that element of original sin that is every person's legacy from the fall of Adam, the first man. In this Calvin was doing no more than repeating elements of the complex theology surrounding the exact nature of Christ that had been the subject of dispute ever since the time of the Early Church, soon after Jesus' death. This, in turn, led him into many further explanations that resulted in a significant proportion of the later editions of the *Institutio* being devoted to a consideration of Jesus and his place in Christianity. It was this, of course, that has allowed some historians to maintain that Jesus was central to Calvin's religious thinking.

This claim does not, however, merely rest on the way in which Calvin saw Jesus as the means by which the elect was justified in the eyes of God. Christ was also of great importance as the vehicle by which God chose to present much of his message to Man. In particular, it was through the words and actions of Jesus that God had taught how His Church should be arranged so as to carry out its twin functions of glorifying His name and nurturing the faith of its members. Without the guidance given by Jesus, mankind would be like a ship adrift at sea without a rudder.

5 The Church

It would be difficult to exaggerate the importance Calvin attached to the Church. He viewed it as the most significant aspect of mankind's life on earth. He described the relationship of the Church to its members as being parallel to the relationship of a mother to her offspring. Just as the mother conceives, bears in her womb, gives birth to and suckles her children, without all of which there could be no mortal life, so the Church provides the only route to eternal life by giving its members both the opportunity to grow in faith by learning about God and His purposes, and a way of serving God in the way He intended. He was in no doubt that anybody who separated himself from the Church could not claim to be a Christian, and he was savage in his condemnation of the various Anabaptist leaders who proclaimed that the Church was an invention of mankind and therefore unnecessary.

1 In as much as God wills that we should preserve the communion
   of His Church, by conversing in the company of the Church such
   as we see it among us, whoever separates himself from it is in
   great danger of withdrawing himself from the communion of the
5 saints.

He therefore went to great lengths to point out that he was in no way separating himself from the Church, however it might appear and however his actions might be represented by Catholic apologists. His version of events was quite clear. As far as he was concerned, it was the Church of Rome that had drifted away from the true Church as established by the disciples of Jesus, because it had lost sight of the will of God and had allowed itself to fall into countless abuses, largely because it had attempted to serve the earthly aims of its leaders. As it was clear to him that the Catholic Church was beyond redemption, he was left with no alternative but to re-establish the true Church of the Early Fathers in the best way he could. Thus, his argument was that it was the Catholics, not the Protestants, who were the destroyers of true Christian unity.

He was aware, of course, that the Church he was building in Geneva, where the population never exceeded 20,000 during his lifetime, was only a minute enterprise in relation to the whole of Christendom. And he did not expect that the relative significance of his Genevan Church would change. Certainly he did not assume that the whole of Protestant Europe would accept all his teachings – nor, of course, did it. So he was prepared to concede that the true Church he was attempting to create in Geneva would not be the only true Church there was. It must be remembered that he lived in a time when each locality was virtually independent politically, despite the emergence of many nascent nation states and other large political units. Unsurprisingly, therefore, his conception was not of a monolithic Church, but of a large number of linked local Churches, all sharing the features that marked them out as true Churches, but possibly differing widely in matters that were not of crucial importance.

* He was consistently certain of the two vital and unnegotiable features that true Churches shared. For a Church to be a true Church, it had to base its teachings exclusively on the Bible, and it had to celebrate the sacraments in a pure manner. This, of course, could have been just another way of Calvin saying that no Church could be a true Church unless it agreed with him. But this is not what he was doing. He was quite prepared to accept other Protestant Churches as being true Churches provided they realistically claimed to base their teachings exclusively on the Bible and recognised only those sacraments that sprang directly from the words of the Bible, even if their interpretations of Scripture did not agree in every detail with his own. So he had no difficulty in accepting the validity of the main Protestant Churches, the Lutherans, the Zwinglians, and the later developers such as the Anglicans. His words were explicit:

1 We ought not to reject any assembly which entertains the pure ministry of the Word and the pure manner of administering the sacraments even though it be defective in several ways. What is more, there may be some defects either in the doctrine or in the
5 manner of administering of the sacraments, which ought not in any way to alienate us from the communion of a Church. For not all the articles of the doctrine of God are of one and the same kind. The knowledge of some of them is so necessary that no-one can doubt them, any more than the decrees or principles of
10 Christianity; as, for example, that Jesus Christ is God and Son of God; that our redemption depends on his mercy alone; and others like them. But there are others again that are in dispute between the Churches, without, however, disrupting their union.

But he was not always so tolerant of differences. For instance, he did from time to time seriously doubt whether a Church could be regarded as a true Church if it did not operate a proper system of discipline. Had he employed this criterion, of course, there would have been few besides the Church of Geneva which would have been acceptable to him.

* Behind all Calvin's thinking about the Church lay an assumption that was an integral part of Christian theological tradition. This was the distinction between the Church visible and the Church invisible. All mainline Christian teachers agree that the real Church of God was the Church invisible, made up of all those souls, in whichever period of history they lived their mortal lives, who had come to God through Jesus and were therefore saved. There was, of course, considerable disagreement about how membership of the Church invisible was gained. The Catholics generally taught that it was by good works, the Lutherans that it was by faith, the Calvinists that it was via election by God, and various Anabaptists that it was by an infusion of saving grace direct from Jesus. But all agreed that without Christ's intervention in some form or other, salvation could not take place. All but the Anabaptists also agreed that the membership of the Church invisible would only be known to others than God on Judgement Day, and that in the meantime there could be no certain identification.

This inability, in Calvin's terms, to separate the elect from the reprobate with certainty during earthly life led all the major organised Protestant groups to teach that it is to the Church visible that one should turn one's attention in practice. Throughout the sixteenth century it was generally assumed by both religious and political leaders that the Church visible should, if possible, include the whole community. It was considered to be totally unacceptable for individuals or groups to attempt to turn their backs on the locally recognised form of organised religion. Hence, of course, much of the violent opposition to the Anabaptists with their separatist tendencies. Thus laws existed, not only in Geneva but throughout most of Europe, to enforce the greatest possible degree of religious conformity, and the expulsion or execution of those who refused to abide by them.

Yet few thinkers shared with Calvin his strength of feeling about the need to exclude from fellowship, and especially from the key sacrament of the Lord's Supper, those members of the community who were thought not to be worthy (see page 17). This was probably because most other religious and political thinkers laid great emphasis on what organised religion could contribute to the individual citizen and to the political community as a whole, as the provider of what was necessary for salvation and much of the social 'cement' necessary to ensure the continuation of 'civilisation'. In such circumstances, there was much to be lost and little to be gained by emphasising disunity by excluding individuals or groups from religious communion with the remainder of the community. But for Calvin one of the major functions of the

Church was to provide a framework within which the Name of God could be glorified. He was convinced that to allow those who were clearly unworthy, in that they were antagonistic to the will of God, to partake in the Lord's Supper was to profane God's Name, and he devoted much of his energy in Geneva to persuading those in authority to ensure that this did not happen. Calvin believed that the prime purpose of the Church visible was to serve God, and he acted accordingly. Many other Protestant leaders at least implied that the Church's main duty was to meet the needs of its members. This was a significant distinction.

6 The Sacraments

Emphasised throughout Calvin's writings on the Church was the great importance he attached to the sacraments. In this he agreed with the Lutherans and the Catholics. But there the similarity with the Catholics ended. Whereas they taught that the sacraments were the vehicle through which God transmitted his grace to mankind, Calvin, like Luther, totally rejected this view. Equally, Calvin joined the other leading Protestants in maintaining that all but two of the seven traditional sacraments of the Catholics were invalid in that they were not based directly on the explicit teachings of Jesus. (For a full discussion of this point see *Luther and the German Reformation*, page 40, in this series.) He was therefore only prepared to recognise the Lord's Supper (variously known as the Mass, the Eucharist, and Holy Communion), and Baptism as proper sacraments.

Calvin's reasons for stressing the importance of the sacraments so strongly are not immediately apparent. He describes them as being:

1 an outward sign by which the Lord seals on our consciences the promises of His good will towards us in order to sustain the weakness of our faith; and we in turn attest our piety towards Him in the presence of the Lord and of His angels and before 5 men.

He further asserts that it is:

1 the surest rule of the sacraments that we should see spiritual things in physical, as if set before our eyes. For the Lord was pleased to represent them by such figures, not because such graces are bound and enclosed in the sacrament so as to be 5 conferred upon us by its power, but only because the Lord, by this token, attests His will towards us.

It is probable that, like Luther, he viewed the celebration of the sacraments as the way in which it was possible to draw closest to Jesus.

It was therefore of high spiritual value, and much to be cherished. In this he was less successful in convincing the citizens of Geneva than in most things. For more than a quarter of a century, he attempted to persuade them that the Lord's Supper was such a vital part of worship that it should be celebrated during every Sunday service or, at the very least, once in each month. But he was unable to win the argument and had to be satisfied with the widely established Protestant practice of celebrating the sacrament at three-monthly intervals. He was, however, able to insist that it was important that children were publicly baptised at the earliest possible opportunity.

* Calvin came to prominence, of course, after Zwingli's death, and therefore missed participating in the great controversy about the Eucharist while it was at its height in the 1520s. But the disagreements still rumbled on throughout his lifetime and he could have resurrected much of the dispute had he so desired. Perhaps it was symptomatic of the fact that he belonged to the second generation of reformers that he was not greatly perturbed by the issue that had seemed so vitally significant to his reforming forebears. He had his own strongly held views on the subject, and these he expounded at length, but without the acrimony that had typified the exchanges between Luther and Zwingli. Certainly he was not prepared to follow Luther's example and pronounce himself unable to accept that those who disagreed with him were members of the true Church. His only demand was that all true Christians should reject the Catholic doctrine of transubstantiation (the belief that the bread and wine used in the Eucharist changed, in essence, into the flesh and blood of Jesus during the celebration of the sacrament), which he regarded as being little more than an appeal to people's primitive belief in magic, introduced by the Church of Rome in the middle ages as a way of strengthening the authority of the priesthood. As long as this happened, he was not greatly excited by disagreements about the exact nature of Jesus' presence during the sacrament.

It is normally said that Calvin tended more towards Zwingli's view than towards Luther's. It is undoubtedly true that he remained unpersuaded by Luther's argument that Jesus was physically present in the bread and wine in the same way as fire (then regarded to be an chemical element) was present in red-hot iron, although the iron was still iron. But this was not surprising, as even Luther's closest supporters found it difficult to appear consistently enthusiastic about their leader's teaching on this subject. But it is not clear that he was really any nearer to Zwingli's view, which rejected the idea of physical presence and stressed that the sacrament was purely symbolic, with Jesus being present in the hearts of the participants as long as they were true believers. It would perhaps be more accurate to suggest that Calvin's real views lay mid-way between the positions adopted by the two protagonists of the 1520s. He summarised his teaching on the issue of Jesus' presence at the Lord's Supper by proclaiming that when Jesus 'bids me take, eat and drink his body and blood under the symbols of bread and wine, I do not doubt that he himself truly presents them, and that I receive them'. But he preferred to teach his followers that here was an issue over which they should not become sidetracked. They should not spend too much time attempting to explain it: rather they should be filled with wonder at its mystery.

1   I am not happy with those persons who, whilst recognising that we have some communion with Christ, when asked to show what it is, make us partakers of the Spirit only, omitting mention of flesh and blood . . . Rather I urge my readers not to confine their
5   mental horizons too narrowly but to strive much higher than I can lead them. For whenever this matter is discussed, when I have tried to say everything, I feel I have yet said little; in proportion to its worth . . . Therefore, nothing remains but to break forth in wonder at this mystery, which plainly neither the mind is able to
10   conceive nor the tongue to express.

Luther, in fact, was alone in attaching such great importance to the detail of teachings on the Eucharist. His followers were mostly less interested in preserving the fine distinctions that their leader struggled to maintain. Calvin was thus in the mainstream of Protestant thinking in taking a somewhat relaxed attitude on the issue.

7 Conclusion

No-one would seriously dispute the claim that John Calvin was one of the handful of leading theologians during the European Reformation. Nor would there be disagreement over the judgement that he was unique in his ability to organise the disparate mass of Protestant teachings into one coherent body, and to present it in such a way that it was readily accessible to all serious-minded and intelligent 'seekers after truth'. This was a huge achievement, and one that was very influential in the subsequent development of Protestantism. But controversy continues over the issue of the originality of his theological work. It is not so much that any case could be made for Calvin as a generator of totally new ideas, but that there is disagreement about the fact that many of those with whom he is sometimes unflatteringly compared were probably no more creative themselves. There is perhaps the danger of assuming that the outstanding administrator and man of business could not also have been the person to move forward the frontiers of thinking on his subject. It smacks of the now discredited, and uniquely British, fallacy that children are either good with their brains or with their hands.

Calvin's thinking and teaching was not, of course, restricted to matters religious. Much of what he had to say related directly to political, social and economic issues. It is to these aspects of his thinking that the next chapter is devoted, although Calvin would have been unhappy at making such a division himself. As far as he was concerned, religion had to do with all areas of thought and behaviour. His view of life was undeniably theocentric (God centred).

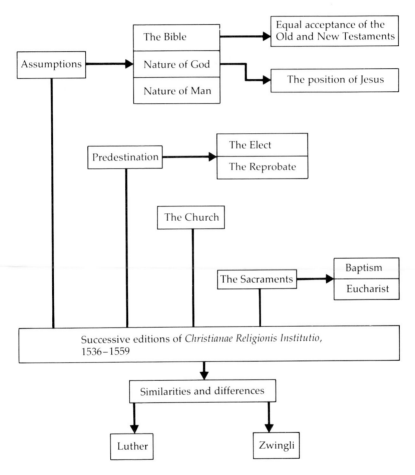

Summary – Calvin's Religious Thinking

Making notes on 'Calvin's Religious Thinking'

When you make notes on this chapter you must keep in mind the main things you are attempting to learn from it. First and foremost, you are trying to understand the main elements of Calvin's religious thinking. On each issue you need to establish in your mind a clear answer to the question, 'What did Calvin think/teach about this?' At the same time you will be considering the 'historiographical dimension', and finding answers to the questions, 'Are/were historians in general agreement about this?' The third question to ask yourself on each issue is, 'To what extent did Calvin differ from other theologians (especially Luther and Zwingli) on this?'

The following headings, sub-headings and questions will help you to organise your notes effectively:

1.   Introduction
1.1. Calvin's place in the theology of the Reformation
1.2. Possible misunderstandings
1.3. *Christianae Religionis Institutio*
2.   Assumptions
2.1. The status of the Bible
2.2. The nature of God
2.3. The nature of Man
2.4. The relationship between God and Man
3.   Predestination
3.1. Calvin's teachings
3.2. Free will. What was double predestination, and why was it important?
4.   The place of Jesus Christ
4.1. Differing views. In what ways have Calvin's teachings been a cause of controversy?
5.   The Church
5.1. The importance of the Church
5.2. True Churches. How did a Church qualify to be considered as a true Church?
5.3. The Church visible and the Church invisible
6.   The sacraments
6.1. The importance of the sacraments
6.2. The Eucharist

Source-based questions on *'Calvin's Religious Thinking'*

1 Calvin's teaching on reprobation
Read carefully the three extracts from the *Institutio* given on pages 47 and 48. Answer the following questions:
a) What argument does Calvin use to support his contention that the reprobate are not blameless for their damnation? Use evidence from the first and third extracts in your answer.
b) Do you find this argument convincing? Explain your answer.

c) To which particular teaching of Calvin's does the second extract mostly relate? Explain your answer.
d) What evidence do the extracts contain of Calvin's assumptions about God's motives?
e) Why did Calvin's teaching on reprobation attract so much opposition?
f) What general differences have developed between Catholic and Calvinist societies largely as a result of their belief or non-belief in predestination?

2 Calvin's teaching on the Church

Read carefully the two extracts from the *Institutio* given on pages 51 and 52. Answer the following questions:
a) What is the significance of the phrase 'such as we see it' in line 2 of the first extract?
b) What is the meaning of the second half of the first extract (from 'whoever' onwards)?
c) What are the limits of toleration laid down by Calvin in the second extract?
d) What evidence do the extracts contain to support the view that Calvin was in favour of Church unity?
e) Describe the 'tone' adopted by Calvin in the two extracts. What does this suggest about his attitude towards his audience?
f) In what ways did Calvin's teachings on the Church differ from Luther's?

3 Calvin's teaching on the sacraments

Read carefully the two extracts from the *Institutio* given on page 54, and answer the following questions:
a) What two purposes do the sacraments fulfil, as described by Calvin in the first extract?
b) On what controversy is Calvin commenting in the second extract?
c) What point of view is he rejecting in the second half of the second extract (from 'not because' onwards)?
d) How would you describe the level of difficulty of these extracts? What does your answer suggest about Calvin as a populariser of ideas?
e) What opinions about the sacraments did the leading Protestant theologians hold in common? What were the aspects over which they disagreed?

4 Calvin and the Eucharist

Read carefully the three brief extracts from the *Institutio* given on page 56, and answer the following questions:
a) Each extract contains one main idea. Describe the three ideas in your own words.

b) Who was the most important of 'those persons' (line 1)?
c) Would you consider Calvin's to be a 'closely reasoned argument'? Explain your answer.
d) Describe the 'tone' adopted by Calvin in these three extracts. What does this suggest about his attitude towards his audience? (Compare your answer to that you gave in 2 e) above.)
e) Based on evidence from these extracts, why did Calvin not particularly wish to engage in major controversy about the Eucharist?
f) What importance did Calvin attach to the Lord's Supper? Support your answer with evidence about his work in Geneva.

CHAPTER 5

Politics, Society and the Economy

Calvin would have objected strongly had anyone suggested to him that his thinking and teachings could be grouped into religious, political, social and economic divisions. As far as he was concerned, all aspects of his work had to do with religion. He assumed that religion affected the totality of living, not just one slice of it, as is the normal modern belief. Questions such as, 'What role should the Church play in politics?' would not have made as much sense to him as they do to us. He viewed what we classify as politics, sociology and economics merely as aspects of religion, in that he believed that all aspects of life were under God's control. But this should not prevent us from considering his teachings and influence under headings that conform to our divisions of knowledge and experience, as long as we do not lose sight of either the essential unity of his thinking, or the fact that he did not divide experience into distinct subject areas as we tend to.

1 Politics

In the mid-sixteenth century there were many more western Europeans who were deeply religious than there are today. But it would be a grave error to imagine that, during the Reformation, religion was the prime motivating force in the lives of the overwhelming majority of the population. Calvin's experiences in Geneva strongly suggest that this was not so. Many people who were seemingly devout and serious-minded about religion were far from being idealists. They were quite prepared to put greed, self-interest, desire for power and advancement, and fear of retribution before religious scruples. This is not to say that they were hypocrites and charlatans – although many were – but merely to state that an increasing number of people were able to compartmentalise their experience in a way that Calvin and the large body of his ardent followers could not. They were prepared to assign religion an important but not over-riding role in their lives.

This was particularly the case among the ruling classes in western European society. For many of them, religion was viewed from a political standpoint rather than vice versa. The question they asked themselves when faced by the possibility of changes in religion was not, 'Will the changes lead to a purified form of religion?' but, 'What will be the effect of the changes on the current distribution of political power?' Their major concern was the possible breakdown of law and order, and the consequent destruction of civilised life as they understood it. There was a general recognition among the landowners of the countryside and the richer merchants and traders of the towns and cities that riot and rebellion on the part of the poorer classes was a constant and frightening danger. This fear was shared, often in a more exaggerated form, by the nobles, princes and kings who were at or near the top of the social and political ladders. They saw religion as a powerful force in maintaining the status quo. The Church had taught for centuries that rulers were God's appointed agents and that to go against their authority was to commit a terrible sin. That the teaching had been effective is shown by the numerous examples of kings, almost unattended, quelling riots and rebellions, and persuading large gatherings of malcontents (described as rabbles or armies depending on one's point of view) to disperse peacefully.

One of the major arguments used in an attempt to discredit Martin Luther in the early years of his struggle with the Church authorities was that in rejecting lawful authority he was encouraging others to do likewise. 'Where will it all end?' was the fear that was being played upon. Luckily for Luther, one of the major uprisings of the century, the Peasants' War of 1524–25 in Germany, broke out within a few years of his rise to prominence, and he was provided with an opportunity to show convincingly that his allegiance lay with the established political and social authorities. Without this unequivocal stance on the duty of the subject to obey his lord, Luther would have found few if any princes willing to follow his religious lead. A similar approach was followed by Ulrich Zwingli in Zurich which, in part, explains the acceptability of his programme of religious reform. This was in marked contrast to the teachings of the many and varied Anabaptist groups, all of which stressed the importance of the direct link between God and the individual believer, and the need to follow the dictates of conscience when they were in conflict with the law of the land or the wishes of the ruler. They taught that the will of God must take precedence over merely manmade obligations. It is therefore not surprising that no hereditary rulers were prepared either to join the Anabaptists or to long tolerate their presence within their territories.

  * Thus it was a matter of crucial importance for Calvin to make clear exactly where he stood on this issue. If he were to support the stance of the Anabaptists, his teachings were almost certain to be outlawed throughout Europe. If he followed the example set by Luther and Zwingli there was the possibility that somewhere his theology would win official approval. It would have been in keeping with his generally narrow view of what constituted moral behaviour for him to base his teachings about the duties of the subject towards his master entirely on a consistent interpretation of Biblical texts, without there being any suspicion that pragmatism (making decisions to secure the best practical outcome, rather than being guided by what one believes to be right) was influencing his judgement. But such was not the case. During the latter years of his life the emphasis in his teachings changed,

and it is impossible to escape the conclusion that this occurred largely as a result of the huge amount of pressure that was applied to him because of the political situation in France. In the process he allowed himself to be manipulated by people who could justly be accused of political opportunism.

Up to the late 1550s, Calvin generally followed the approach adopted by Luther, but with some significant variations. His thinking flowed from his teachings on the essential sinfulness of man. It seemed obvious to him that God had established a system of temporal power exercised by magistrates (the name he used to describe all secular authorities whether they were emperors, kings, princes or councillors) so that people's evil actions could be punished. Equally obvious was the Christian's obligation towards the magistrate:

> 1 The Lord has not only testified that the office of magistrate is
> approved by and acceptable to Him, but He also sets out its dig-
> nity with the most honourable titles and marvellously commends
> it to us . . . they have a mandate from God, having been invested
> 5 with divine authority, and are wholly God's representatives acting
> as what might be called his vice-regents. This is no subtlety of
> mine, but Christ's explanation.

In Calvin's view, this clearly implied obligation was not to cease if a magistrate acted badly:

> 1 We must be very careful not to despise or violate that authority of
> magistrates, full of venerable majesty, which God has established
> by the weightiest decrees, even though it may reside with the
> most unworthy men, who defile it as much as they can through
> 5 their own wickedness. For if the correction of unbridled
> despotism is the Lord's to avenge, let us not at once think that He
> has entrusted it to us, to whom no command has been given
> except to obey and suffer . . . Indeed, He says that those who rule
> for the public benefit are true patterns and evidence of His
> 10 beneficence; and those who rule unjustly and incompetently have
> been raised up by Him to punish the wickedness of the people;
> that all equally have been endowed with that holy majesty with
> which He has invested lawful authority.

This would seem at first sight to be a clear statement of support for governmental action, right or wrong, of the type that made Lutheran-ism so attractive to many rulers who were attempting to establish their authority more firmly or more widely. But it was not as simple as that. While Calvin was obviously close to Luther's basic position, and in common with him launched uncompromising attacks on the teachings of the Anabaptists, he did lay down definite boundaries to the magistrate's authority. He was certainly not prepared to see the Church subservient to the civil power, as Luther and Zwingli were. Magistrates were only to be obeyed as long as they restricted themselves to the aspects of life over which God had given them authority.

> 1 There is a twofold government in man: one aspect is spiritual, whereby the conscience is instructed in piety and reverence towards God; the second is political, whereby man is educated for the duties of humanity and citizenship that must be maintained
> 5 among men . . . The one we may call the spiritual kingdom, the other, the political kingdom . . . There are in men, so to speak, two worlds, over which different kings and different laws have an authority.

Calvin, of course, attempted to put these teachings into practice in Geneva, although the extent to which he managed to implement a policy of clearly divided powers is certainly a matter of dispute (see pages 33–35).

* Unfortunately for Calvin he was not allowed to leave the matter here. His followers abroad frequently pressed him for guidance on whether there were any circumstances in which it was justifiable to actively resist the actions of a magistrate. In particular they were thinking of a magistrate – such as the king of France – who was persecuting God's people (Calvinists) and hindering the establishment of the Church and the conduct of its proper business. At first Calvin was clear and consistent, giving the advice that no more than passive resistance could be offered. In 1556 he wrote in a letter to a French church:

> 1 I have heard that some are debating among themselves whether, if an atrocity is committed against them, they would resort to violence rather than allow themselves to be hunted down by brigands. I beseech you, beloved brethren, to abandon any such
> 5 notions for they will never obtain God's blessing and will never succeed since He disapproves of such things. I well understand what distress you feel, but it is not in my power – nor that of any living creature – to grant you dispensation to act in opposition to the will of God.

But as the pressures on him grew, with hundreds of his followers in France being executed, he gradually shifted his ground. The loophole he used was the existence of various levels of magistracy. Building on arguments that had been employed in Germany to justify the action of the Protestant princes in defying the emperor, he came to the conclusion that popularly elected lower-level magistrates had a duty to resist the tyrannical actions of their superiors.

1 If there are any magistrates appointed by the people to moderate
  the power of kings – . . . such power as the three estates exercise
  in every realm where they hold their chief assemblies – I am so far
  from forbidding them to withstand, in accordance with their
5 duty, the violence and cruelty of kings that, if they connive with
  kings in their oppression of their people, then I declare they are
  guilty of the most wicked perfidy, because they dishonestly betray
  the freedom of the people, of which they know that they have
  been appointed protectors by God's law.

Thus was born the Calvinist doctrine that resistance could be offered
to persecution as long as it was led by people holding official positions
of authority, which, of course, seemed to open the floodgates of
rebellion. It signalled to the rulers of states with Calvinist minorities
that they were indeed facing a serious threat to their authority, and
perhaps even to their very existence. This appeared to be proved in
1560 when it was widely reported that Calvin had given his blessing to a
conspiracy aimed at placing the young king of France under the control
of Calvinist nobles. But, in fact, Calvin had not agreed that *armed*
resistance was acceptable. Nor was he ever to do so. All he did was to
become suitably vague over where the borderline of allowable
behaviour lay, so that less scrupulous followers could mis-represent
him with impunity. In this way he was able to content himself with the
thought that he had remained true to his earlier beliefs, while at the
same time allowing others to secure the outcome that they desired.
After his death in 1564, Theodore Beza from Geneva, and local leaders
such as John Knox in Scotland, completed the transformation of
Calvinism from a faith that believed in meekly accepting persecution to
one that became renowned for actively resisting it.
  * It is therefore not surprising that Calvinism became identified with
revolution and radical political thinking. It was looked upon as the
enemy of monarchy and the friend of republicanism. In part this was a
natural consequence of the fact that Geneva was its birthplace and
remained its headquarters throughout the sixteenth century, during
which time the republican city-state resisted all attempts to bring it
back under the control of its previous princely ruler, the Duke of
Savoy. This tendency was encouraged by the emergence of the United
Provinces (Holland) as an independent Calvinist republic in the early
seventeenth century, particularly as it was born following a long and
bloody struggle to overthrow its rightful ruler, the king of Spain. But it
should not be assumed from this that Calvin was a political
revolutionary – although it is equally clear that he was not a natural
conservative, as was Martin Luther. His summary of his political stance
shows that in no sense was he a radical nor even a genuine democrat:

1 Obviously it is idle for men in private life, who are disqualified

from deliberating upon the organisation of any commonwealth, to dispute over what would be the best kind of government in the place where they live . . . If the three forms of government which
5 the philosophers discuss are considered in isolation, I will not deny that aristocracy, or a system compounded of aristocracy and democracy, far excels all the others: not indeed in itself, but because it is very rare for kings so to control their will that it never is at variance with what is just and right; or for them to have been
10 endowed with sufficient prudence and shrewdness to know how much is enough. Therefore man's weakness causes it to be safer for a number of men to exercise government so that each one can help, teach and admonish the other.

2 Society

For many people the two words 'Calvinism' and 'Puritanism' naturally associate together. That is not to suggest that all Puritans were Calvinists, for there were many Puritan groups, especially in the seventeenth century, who laid no claim to be followers of Calvin's teachings. But it is generally accepted that the opposite was true – that all Calvinists were Puritans, and that this was one of the major distinguishing factors between them and the other Protestant groups such as the Lutherans and Zwinglians.

The main elements of the Puritanism that Calvin struggled so hard to put into practice in Geneva all had to do with the way in which the individual lived his daily life. It sprang from his emphasis on the sinfulness of man and the belief that it was reasonable for God to punish people by making their lives on earth generally unpleasant. This thinking was reinforced by the assumption that the purpose of life was to glorify the Name of God, and that this could best be done by carrying out the instructions that he had laid down in his revelation to mankind, the Bible. But whereas Luther taught that if an activity was not specifically forbidden in the Scriptures it was acceptable unless it was clearly harmful to others, Calvin generally taught that the true Christian should only do things that were positively approved of in the Bible. This distinction had dramatic effects. Whereas in Lutheran communities it was not frowned upon to do things merely for pleasure , those in Calvinist societies who sought to enjoy themselves were looked upon as reprobates and people to be shunned.

Some caution must, however, be exercised in attributing all of this to the personal influence of Calvin. Although he was clearly the driving force behind the establishment of a Puritanical society in Geneva (see pages 29–32), he was at times uneasy that the enthusiasm of his followers was carrying matters further than he really wished them to go. He would certainly have been very perturbed had he lived to witness the extremes to which some Calvinist communities took his teachings, especially in Scotland and in the early settlements of New England. But it tells us much about John Calvin the man that he made little effort to correct those who went further than he thought was justified, especially when the excesses were in a direction with which he was emotionally in sympathy. He wrote words of caution to those who were insistent on extreme simplicity of dress, suggesting that they would soon be advocating that everybody be dressed in sack-cloth, but he actually did nothing to prevent them exercising their influence. When his followers in 1550, seemingly without his knowledge or support, successfully sponsored a new regulation in Geneva forbidding the celebration of Christmas, except on the Sunday after 25th December, he made no protest despite the fact that it was extremely unpopular among a large minority of his fellow citizens.

* Calvin and his later followers have often been accused of sexism, in that they relegated women into a second class, semi-servile status. Much of this criticism is justified. It would, of course, be totally anachronistic to judge their actions according to late twentieth century criteria alone, but it is clear that, even given the generally accepted standards of the time, Calvinism was generally harsh and unfair to women. Certainly they were expected meekly to accept male dominance. Calvin set the tone for this within his own family. When he was searching for a wife in 1539 he made it very clear to Farel, whose assistance he sought in the venture, what his priorities were:

1   I am not one of those insane lovers who embrace also the vices of those whom they love so that they are smitten at first sight with a fine figure. The only sort of beauty which attracts me is some one who is chaste, economical, patient, and some one who will (it is to
5   be hoped) be concerned about my health.

Once married he did not treat his wife as a partner and companion, but solely as an especially reliable house-keeper and nurse. The couple had no children. These unchallenged assumptions about what constituted the correct relationship between men and women were part of an outlook on life that attached unspoken blame to women for being the weaker sex. The 'weaker', of course, was viewed in moral, not physical, terms. Eve was not to be forgiven for causing Adam's fall, just as all Jews must share the guilt for the crucifixion of Jesus. Calvin's attitudes are partially revealed in an extract from one of his Genevan sermons:

1   Women have been allowed for a long time to become increasingly audacious. And besides, speech apart, they wear such provocative clothes that it is hard to discern whether they are women or men. They appear in new dresses and trinkets, so that some new
5   disguise is daily to be seen. They come decked out in peacock-tail

fashion, so that a man cannot pass within three feet of them without feeling, as it were, a windmill sail swirling past him. Ribald songs, too, are part of their behaviour.

Yet in one aspect of the treatment of women, Calvin was actually far in advance of the norms of his time. It was almost universally the practice for women to be treated unequally in marriage and matrimonial law. But in Geneva, thanks to Calvin's direct influence, this situation was almost totally corrected.

1 If a husband accuses his wife of adultery and proves it with witnesses of sufficient reliability and asks for a divorce, it shall be granted to him . . . He shall be asked, however, to pardon his wife, but he should not be further constrained if he has made up 5 his mind.
    It used to be the case that the rights of women did not equal those of men in the matter of divorce. However, the words of the apostle make it clear that marriage is reciprocal and a mutual obligation so far as conjugal rights are concerned. Therefore a 10 wife should be no more subject to her husband than a husband to his wife. If a man is convicted of adultery and his wife asks to be separated from him it shall be granted, provided that the partners cannot be mutually reconciled.

This re-balancing of an unequal relationship also extended to dealings between the generations. It was common for marriages in Geneva to be arranged by parents, and not unknown for children to be forced into marriages against their clearly expressed wishes. Calvin was instrumental in changing this situation. The age of majority, at which children could marry without the consent of their parents, was lowered (to 20 for women and 24 for men), and it was made clear that children could not be forced into marriages as minors. But not all that children might have wished was granted:

1 If two young people become engaged to be married without consent – through foolishness or lightheadedness – they are to be punished and reprimanded and the marriage is to be rescinded by those who are in charge of them.
5   If any one is found to have been forced to become betrothed, then those responsible shall spend three days on bread and water and afterwards supplicate the magistrates for clemency.
    If children marry without the permission of their father and mother, but at the permitted age, they shall be accepted as having 10 been married because of the over-rigorous attitude of their father.
In these cases, fathers shall be compelled to provide a dowry or

agree to such terms and conditions [as Genevan laws lay down for dowries] as if they had agreed.

No father can constrain his child to a marriage which seems
15 good to him but has not the wishes and consent of the child.
At the same time, if, having refused one match against paternal wishes, the child should afterwards choose another, which proves less profitable and advantageous, then, because of the previous disobedience and stubbornness, the father should not be required
20 to give the couple anything during his lifetime.

* Calvin's desire to alter the balance of power between husband and wife over divorce, and between parent and child over the selection of marriage partner, should not be taken as proof that he was in any general way a social egalitarian. He was, in fact, just the opposite. He believed that differences in social status were God-given, and were therefore not open to question. To those of his followers who wanted to understand why God had ordered things as He had, he replied that the answer could never be known and the question should never be asked. Good Christians should accept that the social structure was as it was because that was how God, in His infinite wisdom, wished it to be. There the discussion must end. In taking this stance Calvin was not denying himself the opportunity to seek changes that he personally favoured. He was quite content to work within a social structure where the concepts of human rights and equality of opportunity were unknown. His experience had seemed to prove to him that, as different stations in life required different skills and abilities of their holders, God had created men and women of different types. In this he was at one with the vast majority of his contemporaries, who merely saw the working of greed and jealousy in demands for greater social parity. It would be harsh to criticise Calvin for not being interested in the rights of the individual.

Yet one is left uneasy about Calvin's lack of interest in the problems of the poor and the inadequate. At times he seemed almost to celebrate the fact that, in his view, they were as they were because they deserved to be so, and that he and the other leading members of the community had no responsibility for the situation. In this respect he compares very unfavourably with Martin Luther. Admittedly, Luther shared nearly all his assumptions about the God-given nature of social structures and about their implications. But he softened what could have been an unsympathetic stance by stressing the fact that all legitimate callings were of equal value and status in the eyes of God. This belief in the equal intrinsic worth of all human beings was one of the endearing features of Luther, and its lack in Calvin has led historians of the last 150 years (when liberal and humanitarian assumptions have been the norm) to comment on his hardness and lack of warmth. The attempts by his apologists to correct what they see to be an imbalance in history's judgement of Calvin in this respect have been almost entirely unsuccessful.

We are therefore left with a paradox. On the one hand Calvin was a social revolutionary, probably causing as dramatic changes in Genevan daily life as were brought about by any sixteenth century reformer in any situation. On the other hand he was a social reactionary supporting a social structure that most commentators in the late twentieth century would describe as being riddled with abuses and injustices. The explanation lies, of course, in his particular blend of fundamental assumptions about life and its purpose. Given that he placed God at the centre of his map for giving meaning to existence, and refused to allow humanity any place but at the periphery, his stance seems to be full of inconsistencies to those who do not share his starting points. In many ways it was his refusal to compromise his major principles (in almost all situations) that marks him out among the leaders of the Reformation. Many claimed to place God first and Man last in their thinking, but few ended up concentrating so clearly on the needs of God and ignoring so pointedly the needs of Man. But, of course, Calvin's clarity and consistency do not necessarily make his thinking attractive to us. Nor was this his intention.

3 The Economy

Some historians have considered that the most historically significant effect of Calvin and the Calvinists was on attitudes towards the economy and economic activity. This view is particularly associated with the name of Max Weber, who was a social sciences teacher in a German university in the early twentieth century. In two articles (*The Protestant Ethic and the Spirit of Capitalism* and *The Protestant Sects and the Spirit of Capitalism*), written between 1904 and 1906, he elaborated his theory that the development of capitalism owed much to Calvinism. His argument relied heavily on the contention that several of the features which differentiated capitalism from other economic systems can be firmly linked with Protestantism, and with Calvinism in particular. He made much of the Calvinist teachings of the seventeenth and eighteenth centuries which explicitly stated that the generation of ever-increasing amounts of wealth was not only acceptable, but was an obligation placed on the 'elect' by God. He also highlighted the asceticism (strong self-discipline in denying oneself pleasure) that was a feature of most Calvinists, and argued that this encouraged the unceasing struggle for increased wealth as an end in itself. He saw the accumulation of money with no objective in view other than the acquisition of more wealth as being one of the 'unnatural' features of capitalism, but one which does much to explain its success. He maintained that such an unnatural way of behaving could not have arisen spontaneously, and argued that it must have developed out of orthodox Calvinist teaching. His interpretation rapidly caught the imagination of the academic world, and led to a lively debate that lasted for more than 60 years. However, given the very generalised nature of much of the discussion, it is not surprising that no widely accepted conclusion was ever reached.

The most famous of Weber's supporters in Britain was R.H. Tawney, one of the more prominent English-speaking historians of the mid-century period. Tawney, as a Marxist, was especially interested in charting the changes that led to feudalism's replacement by capitalism, for he hoped that a similar sequence of events would lead to the eventual triumph of communism over capitalism. His interpretation was developed in a series of lectures delivered in the early 1920s, and subsequently published in book form as *Religion and the Rise of Capitalism*, one of the most famous historical works of its era. The line taken by Tawney was generally supportive of Weber, although he did criticise him for failing to see that the 'spirit of capitalism' was engendered by Protestantism as a whole and not just by Calvinism, and for understressing the fact that not all aspects of Calvin's teachings were economically progressive.

Tawney's general thesis was that the economic ideas associated with feudalism were gradually replaced by capitalism largely because of the Reformation. He could see that the areas of Europe in which capitalism developed earliest and most strongly largely coincided with the countries in which Protestantism was most influential. He therefore looked for evidence to support Weber's view that this was not merely a coincidence but was a matter of cause and effect. He found most supporting evidence in Calvin's writings and in the actions and attitudes of his later followers. The most convincing evidence appeared to relate to the development of the 'Protestant work ethic'. This phenomenon was most obvious in those communities which were closely associated with Calvin's teachings – Switzerland, Holland, Scotland, England, and the English and Dutch settlements in America.

It seemed to Tawney that Calvinists, from the sixteenth to the nineteenth centuries, had been prepared to work harder and had shown greater initiative and enterprise than members of other religious groups. He explained this in terms of their attitudes and beliefs. Calvinism was characterised by an acceptance of firm discipline and a valuing of action rather than contemplation. It was hostile to the pursuit of pleasure, which, of course, meant that much more time and energy were available for productive labour. Even the very young were taught that 'the devil finds work for idle hands to do'. There was a widespread assumption that to work hard is virtuous and to be idle is sinful. To this could be added the belief in many Calvinist communities that success in work was a sign from God that one was numbered among the elect. Although this belief was never part of Calvin's explicit teachings, it was encouraged by his willingness to accept that God gave signs (but not certainty) to those whom he had chosen for salvation. Many Calvinists, especially members of the professional classes and self-employed artisans and entrepreneurs, struggled hard to be success-ful partly to gain endorsement of their belief that they were among the elect. As time passed by, and certainly by the mid-seventeenth century, most Calvinist groups automatically equated success with worldly wealth. To become rich through one's own efforts was therefore judged to be the surest evidence that salvation lay ahead. The acquisition of more and more money therefore became an honourable activity. Such a change of view was, according to Tawney, just what was necessary for capitalism to replace feudalism as the prevailing economic ideology.

* Within this generalised argument, which spanned the events of several centuries, Tawney also dealt with specifics. He paid particular attention to Calvin's teachings on usury (the lending of money for gain) because he thought that it was the change in attitudes about the funding of trade and industry that encouraged the rise of capitalism and the decline of feudalism. Throughout the Middle Ages the Church had taught that to make profit from the lending of money to others is evil. This approach had been generally accepted as representing Jesus's teaching on the subject, and Christians had mostly avoided breaching this – although, of course, the vast majority of people had no capital to lend in any case. So money lending had mostly been left to the Jews who, by filling the vacuum, had laid themselves open to further hatred and prejudice.

The Church's teaching on usury did not appear strange or unsuitable to most mid-sixteenth century Christians. It was an integral part of a coherent view of the nature of property and its associated rights and responsibilities. This assumed that all good things came from God and were intended for use as he directed. The rich were rich so that they could maintain themselves in the condition to which He had appointed them. But they must not be extravagant. If circumstances led to them having greater resources than they required to pay for what was needed, they should donate the surplus to help any members of the community (usually the poor) who had insufficient to meet their needs. If they did not do this, somebody would of necessity suffer, as it was assumed that God had provided just the right amount for all people's needs to be met. The idea that the total of available wealth might be increasing was unknown. It was therefore not acceptable to build up a reserve of capital, or to seek riches that you did not need.

This, of course, was largely theory, and was completely unworkable in anything but a basic subsistence economy. Once an extensive trade in luxury goods had developed, as it had long before Calvin's time, and once warfare had become extremely expensive because of the develop-ment of costly weapons and materials, government at all levels had to ignore breaches in the Church's code of conduct as long as they were not too blatant and did not directly harm too many people. By Calvin's time, it was accepted in most of the commercial centres of Europe (of which Geneva was one) that the charging of interest on loans, as long as it was not an attempt to benefit from the misfortunes of others, was acceptable provided it was at a reasonable rate. Thus 'usury' came to mean the charging of excessive interest, and it was generally accepted that the reasonable rate should be decided by the local magistrates, who should then ensure that it was not exceeded.

Tawney's contention was that Calvin was more prepared to accept a flexible approach to charging interest on loans than were most other Church leaders, and was positively hostile to the view that the acquisition of personal wealth was sinful. In so doing, Tawney argued, Calvin played a large part in establishing the respectability of capitalism, so removing one of the major obstacles to its successful development. But Tawney relied on evidence that was far from conclusive. He probably greatly overstated the case for considering Calvin as ahead of his time in economic thinking. It is true that Calvin did not object when the Council in Geneva raised the legal rate of interest, or when a bank was established with the specific purpose of lending money at interest (the profits to come to the city). Equally there is no doubting his rejection of the medieval view that merchants were parasites when he wrote in a letter:

What reason is there why the income from business should not be larger than that from landowning? Whence do the merchant's profits come, except from his own diligence and industry?

However, this does not represent as dramatic a shift in the Church's official position as Tawney suggested. Although he was not as restrictive in his views as churchmen had traditionally been, Calvin was by no means a believer in an economic free-for-all. One of his most frequently repeated complaints about the Council in Geneva was that they were insufficiently vigilant in enforcing the various regulations designed to protect the poor from economic exploitation. This approach continued under Beza's leadership. In fact, it was probably the major area of dispute between the Church and the state in Geneva in the generation after Calvin's death. Certainly Calvin was consistent in his condemnation of any activity that put the financial interests of the individual before the economic interests of the community.

1 When the Lord afflicts a country with war or famine, the rich make great gain by such evils. They abuse the scourge of God; for we see merchants getting rich in the midst of wars, inasmuch as they scrape together a booty from every quarter. For those who
5 wage war are forced to borrow cash, as also the peasants and

artisans, so they can pay their taxes; and, then, so that they can live, they are obliged to make unjust agreements . . .

This restricted view of what constituted acceptable economic behaviour was mirrored in many Calvinist communities subsequently. This was particularly so in the early Puritan settlements of New England where strenuous efforts were made to enforce detailed regulations designed to limit economic self-interest. Rules were designed to outlaw such false principles as:

1. That a man might sell as dear as he can, and buy as cheap as he can.
2. If a man lose by casualty of sea, etc., in some of his commodities, he may raise the price of the rest.
3. That he may sell as he bought, though he paid too dear, and though the commodity be fallen, etc.
4. That, as a man may take the advantage of his own skill or ability, so he may of another's ignorance or necessity.

This was far from encouraging the development of the 'enlightened self-interest' which supporters of capitalism suggest is its most striking feature. It was the fact that Calvin and his followers consistently urged the necessity of putting God first, others second, and oneself last in all aspects of life, including economic activity, that makes Weber and Tawney's argument less than totally convincing. There is also the suspicion that they did not do enough to prove the existence of a causal relationship between religion and the rise of capitalism. It is one thing to show that many of the famous entrepreneurs of the two and a half centuries after Calvin's death were Protestants, but quite another to establish that they were successful entrepreneurs *because* they were Protestants. If one were prepared to accept that there is no need to *prove* causal relationships in historical argument, it would even be possible to develop a reasonably convincing interpretation based on the contention that capitalism developed for reasons unrelated to religion, and that it only failed to blossom in some Catholic societies because the Counter-Reformation successfully resisted it. Few serious historians would accept this.

So we are left with an interpretation that is interesting and perceptive, and which undoubtedly has elements of truth to it. But Weber and his supporters seem to have overstated their case (an occupational hazard for historians who attempt to change our view of the past by identifying 'broad-brush' trends that have not previously been widely recognised), and to have ignored other features (such as geographical location and the existence of raw materials) which may have played as large a part as religion in destroying the economic ethos that had prevailed in the Middle Ages. However, the fact that no contemporary historian of note accepts Weber's or Tawney's theses in their original form should not lead us to dismiss them as valueless. They have greatly affected the questions research historians have asked about Protestantism during the past 50 years, and in so doing have done much to shape the framework within which this topic is studied. Weber's and Tawney's writings are clearly landmarks in the study of early modern history.

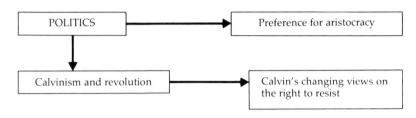

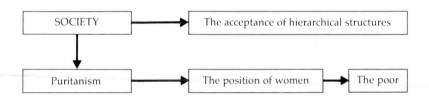

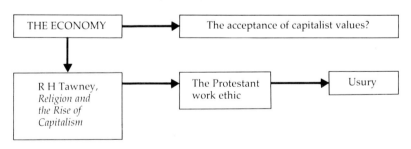

Summary – Politics, Society and the Economy

Making notes on 'Politics, Society and the Economy'

Your main aim in reading this chapter is to build up a clear understanding of Calvin's teachings on political, social and economic matters. Wherever possible you should identify ways in which his teachings were different from Luther's. The following headings and questions should help you to structure your ideas:

1. Politics
1.1. Religion as a control mechanism
1.2. The subject's right to resist his ruler. Why was this issue important?
1.3. Calvin's changing stance on the issue
2. Society
2.1. Puritanism
2.2. Attitudes towards women
2.3. Attitudes towards the structure of society. In what ways were Calvin's views paradoxical?
3. The economy
3.1. Weber and Tawney's general thesis
3.2. Usury
3.3. Assessment. What are the strengths and weaknesses of Weber and Tawney's thesis?

Answering essay questions on 'Calvin's Teachings'

You will need to have a coherent view of the full range of Calvin's thinking, as discussed in the last two chapters. It is not a great help to know about one part and not the other. Nor will it be sufficient to understand Calvin's thinking in isolation. You must be prepared to discuss the similarities and differences between his teachings and those of Luther and, preferably, Zwingli. This is because the majority of questions are of the 'Compare and contrast' type. At its most straightforward the wording will be such as:

1. 'Compare and contrast the teachings of Luther and Calvin,' or,
2. 'In what ways were the teachings of Luther and Calvin (a) similar, and (b) dissimilar?'

You should be carefully prepared for such questions before you meet them, as they are very predictable. Draw up one list of the issues the two men agreed on, and another list of their areas of disagreement. Group them under the four headings *theological, political, economic* and *social*. You will rarely be asked to cover all these areas in one answer. Ensure that you read questions carefully to determine what you should include and what you should omit. What issues would you include in answers to the following questions?

3. 'What was distinctive about Calvin's religious thinking?'
4. 'Compare Calvin and Zwingli as religious reformers.'

5. 'Contrast the views of Luther and Calvin on the relationship that should exist between the Church and the State'.

Source-based questions on 'Politics, Society and the Economy'

1 Calvin on the authority of magistrates
Read carefully the three extracts from Calvin's writings given on pages 63–64. Answer the following questions:
a) What is Calvin's purpose in writing the last sentence of the first extract?
b) What view is Calvin putting forward in the second extract about the way in which tyrants should be treated? What argument does he use to justify this view?
c) What limitation to the magistrate's power is suggested in the third extract?
d) Which of the teachings covered by the three extracts would not have been acceptable to Lutherans and Zwinglians? Explain your answer.
e) Do these extracts support the view that Calvin was a political revolutionary? Explain your answer.

2 Calvin on the right to resist magistrates
Read carefully the extracts from Calvin's letter of 1556 (page 64) and from the 1559 edition of *Christianae Religionis Institutio* (page 65). Answer the following questions:
a) In the first extract Calvin gives two reasons why those who commit atrocities should not be resisted. What are these reasons? Which one is not dependent on a moral argument?
b) In the second extract Calvin explains the duties of 'magistrates appointed by the people to moderate the power of kings'. What are these duties?
c) How far are the views expressed in the two extracts, (i) consistent, and (ii) inconsistent? Justify your answer in detail.
d) Calvin wraps up his meaning in the second extract in a form of words that is not immediately clear. What were likely to have been his reasons for doing this?
e) How reliable are the two extracts as evidence of Calvin's views?

3 Calvin on forms of government
Read carefully the extract given on pages 65–6, and answer the following questions:
a) What main assumption underlies the first sentence of the extract? Explain your answer.
b) What evidence does the extract contain that Calvin had engaged in humanist study?

c) In what ways are the arguments used in the second half of this extract at variance with the arguments used in the extracts given on page 63? What does this variation suggest?

d) What form of government would best fit a Calvinist society? Explain your answer.

4 Calvin on the position of women

Read carefully the four extracts given on pages 67–69. Answer the following questions:

a) What view of women is communicated in the first two extracts? Support your answer with evidence.

b) In the third extract Calvin claims that the rights of women equal the rights of men in divorce. Does the evidence in the extract totally justify this claim? Explain your answer.

c) What assumptions about the purposes of marriage underlie the fourth extract?

d) Did Calvin have a coherent view of women, their rights and their roles? Explain your answer.

e) How far is it justified to criticise Calvin for his attitude towards women?

f) How far would it be accurate to describe Calvinism as 'a socially revolutionary creed'?

5. Calvin on the economy

Read carefully the three extracts given on pages 73–74, and answer the following questions:

a) Explain, in as much detail as possible, the assumptions against which Calvin was arguing in the first extract.

b) What is Calvin attacking in the second extract?

c) Are the views expressed in the second extract at variance with those of the first? Explain your answer.

d) The third extract gives examples of what should *not* be done. Based on the evidence provided by this extract, draw up a list of four positive rules that should be followed by Calvinist merchants and traders. Comment on their practicality.

e) What is meant by 'the Protestant work ethic'? What has been its historical significance?

CHAPTER 6

The Spread of Calvinism

If Calvin had been no more than the Reformer of Geneva he would now be largely forgotten outside Switzerland. The Church he struggled so hard to establish would probably have been subsumed within a wider organisation within a generation or two. His work would be viewed by historians as one of the interesting backwaters of sixteenth century religious history, much as the activities of many of the Anabaptist groups have been. But this did not happen. John Calvin is rightly regarded as one of the two giants of the Reformation. He holds this position largely because his thinking and teachings provided much of the impetus for the further spread of Protestantism in the decades after Martin Luther's death in 1546.

Calvin's rise to international prominence was in no sense automatic. Luther to some extent had greatness thrust upon him as he was the first in the field, but those who came later were likely to be categorised as being no more than his followers. Ulrich Zwingli had suffered in this way and had greatly resented it. (The relationship between Luther and Zwingli is dealt with in *Luther and the German Reformation* in this series.) Calvin was also referred to as a Lutheran during his early years as a reformer, but once he settled in Geneva it was assumed that in practice he would be a Zwinglian. No-one, of course, suspected that he would become a religious leader in his own right. The fact that he did so was the result of a complex set of happenings and situations, only some of which were under his own control.

1 Calvin and the Protestants of Switzerland and Germany

For much of the first half of his time in Geneva, Calvin was regarded by one faction or the other as a useful political pawn. The reform of the Genevan Church had originally been sponsored by Berne whose rulers had recognised that if Geneva remained Protestant it was more likely to fall under its political influence than if it reverted to Catholicism. Yet Berne, which wished to undermine Geneva's independence, was not itself truly independent in religious matters. It generally followed the lead of the Zwinglian Church of Zurich. As a result, it was certainly expected that when Farel was 'lent' to Geneva to spearhead the reform movement there, he would act as if he were a disciple of Zwingli. But it was soon recognised that his assistant, Calvin, was no mere follower of other men. He had ideas of his own and was only prepared to alter them if he could be convinced that they were wrong. In particular, he was unprepared to accept the Zwinglian (and Lutheran) view that the Church should be under the control of the magistrates. It was this issue that led to Farel and Calvin being exiled in 1538 (see page 13). It was also this independence of view that led to Calvin's return three years later, when the anti-Berne faction on the Council saw him as a useful symbol of their refusal to be dominated by their Swiss protectors. So, for political reasons, Calvin was encouraged and supported in his determination to be a religious leader in his own right.

Yet this desire for separate recognition was not at all egotistical. Calvin was no seeker of fame, power or financial reward: his desire was to honour God by ensuring that His instructions to Man were correctly taught. In fact, he would have been genuinely pleased had it been possible for him to fade quietly into the background. But, as he was driven by a conscience that rarely allowed him to compromise a principle in order to avoid a fight, he was kept constantly in the limelight. Given this attitude, it was remarkable that he tried as hard as he did to seek agreement with other Protestants, especially in Switzerland. Unlike the leading Protestants in Germany, many of whom continued to seek agreement with the Catholics as late as the 1550s, he limited his aspirations to a possible reconciliation and mutual recognition of the major Protestant groupings. While he was in exile in Strasbourg he had become convinced of the impossibility of reaching agreement with the Catholics. He had attended series of meetings called by the Emperor at which efforts had been made to identify the common ground on which there could be a re-unification of the Church. These had persuaded him that the Catholics would never be prepared to compromise on vital issues such as the invalidity of any teachings or practices that were not based on the Bible. However, he was unprepared to accept that the failure of Luther and Zwingli to agree at the Marburg Colloquy in 1529 should necessarily mean that the Protestant Churches would always remain divided.

* At the outset Calvin was not in a strong position to act as a mediator between the Lutherans and the Zwinglians. The Zwinglians, in particular, were very suspicious of him and tended to regard him as a dangerous renegade. There was even for a time a concerted attempt by the Church leaders of Berne to discredit him and secure his expulsion from Geneva. But the churchmen of Zurich were more prepared to accept him. This was partly because they were more distant than Berne, and had no vested political interest in seeking his downfall, and partly because they were led by Heindrich Bullinger, Zwingli's successor and a man of stature whom Calvin could respect and who could respect Calvin in return. Apart from Calvin, Bullinger was the most influential of the second generation of Protestant leaders. His advice was sought by most of the Protestant rulers of the time. Calvin rapidly established a *rapport* with him and the two men corresponded frequently and frankly. This provided Calvin with an opportunity to enter into negotiations with Bullinger over a common statement of beliefs for the two Churches. He hoped that mutual support and recognition would be

extended to all churches which accepted it. The venture achieved success in 1549 when the *Consensus Tigurinus* (Agreement of Zurich) was signed, essentially between Zurich and Geneva, but subsequently accepted by all the Swiss Protestant churches. However, it is something of a paradox that Calvin, who was ferocious even over quite minor matters of detail in internal Genevan church affairs, was responsible for initiating the *Consensus Tigurinus* which was imprecise on matters of major importance. In fact, he planned that it should be loosely worded in places so that areas of possible disagreement would be blurred. He was even prepared to accept that it would be inconsistent in the way in which it dealt with some of the most hotly disputed points. It seems that he was, after all, enough of a politician to realise that agreements between autonomous groups are rarely arrived at without some compromises and deliberate vagueness. He was clearly prepared to go to some lengths to establish a united front among the major Protestant churches.

* Calvin had hopes that the *Consensus Tigurinus* would form the basis of an agreement between the Swiss Protestant churches and the Lutherans of Germany. For many years he had been on very good terms with Philip Melanchthon, Martin Luther's closest colleague and disciple. Melanchthon was probably the clearest thinking and academically most able of the leading Lutherans, but unfortunately he was distrusted by many of his colleagues who considered him to be too open-minded and too willing to change his views in order to secure agreements with other churches. His openly admitted dedication to the task of re-uniting the whole of Christendom was resented by those who saw their main task as the safeguarding of the purity of Lutheranism, especially after their founder's death in 1546. Melanchthon was therefore not universally recognised as his leader's successor, as had happened with Bullinger in Zurich and was to happen with Beza in Geneva. In fact there was a considerable and acrimonious dispute among the Lutherans about the direction in which their Church was to go. The outcome was that the Philipists (as Melanchthon's supporters were called), with their willingness to consider amending their standpoint in order to reach agreement with either the Catholics or the Calvinists, became increasingly discredited. The leadership of the Lutheran movement passed into the hands of men who were keen to emphasise the points that marked out their Church as being different. They had no desire to reach agreement with others. As Calvin wrote in frustration, 'The chief obstacle to agreement with the Lutherans is the powerful hold exercised by the preconceptions, accepted for so long that people are not prepared to consider anything new'.

One Lutheran leader in particular, Joachim Westphal, saw it as his duty to stress the ways in which Calvin and the Lutherans differed, and to make it impossible for there to be any reconciliation between them. While he was the leading minister in the North German city of

Hamburg, he carried on Luther's tradition of launching vitriolic attacks on his opponents, among whom he numbered Calvin. At first Calvin attempted to answer his verbal assaults, but he soon came to realise that the man was not to be reasoned with. However it was with considerable sadness that in doing so he accepted that there would be no agreement among the Protestants to live in peace and harmony with one another. He was particularly disappointed because he felt that their disagreements were mainly caused by differences in emphasis rather than by a failure to agree on major doctrinal issues.

In his dealings with his fellow Protestants in Switzerland and Germany, Calvin was not attempting to convert them to his beliefs. His aim was merely to secure agreement on the irreducible minimum that was sufficient for a church to be accepted among the body of Reformed Churches. He hoped that once such an agreement was reached, Protestants would no longer waste time and energy in squabbling among themselves: attention could be devoted to defeating what he believed to be the work of the Devil, the Church of Rome. It is therefore not surprising that Calvinism did not make great inroads into areas where Protestant Churches were already firmly established.

Yet there were some notable exceptions. In the decades following Luther's death in 1546, parts of Germany experienced what historians have called a Second Reformation. The impetus for this came from a small number of princes who became convinced that Luther had accepted a number of Catholic beliefs and practices without proper Biblical authority. They instructed their Churches to amend what they were teaching and doing. But they were not slavish followers of Calvin, although they were greatly influenced by his theology and his teachings on Church discipline. They took from his teachings those elements that seemed particularly appropriate to their situations. The hub of this Second Reformation in Germany was the Palatinate, one of the more powerful states in the south. The capital, Heidelberg, became the local equivalent of Geneva after 1561. Preachers and publications were sent out in considerable numbers, and guidance was given to Calvinist communities in neighbouring states. However, the most significant support provided by the Palatinate was political. The local ruler, the Elector, as one of the leading princes of the Empire, was able to act as the advocate for the Calvinist cause in the highest political circles. He was also able to offer his co-religionists armed support when they were under attack, as he did in both France and the Netherlands to great acclaim, although to little practical effect.

The statistics relating to Calvinism in Germany can be misleading. Although twenty eight states became Calvinist at one time or another, many of them were so tiny that they were insignificant. Others were described as being Calvinist, but in reality were as close to Lutheranism as they were to the situation in Geneva. In the late sixteenth century the impression was given internationally that Calvinism was an important force in Germany. This owed much to propaganda and Catholic rulers' willingness to believe the worst, and does not hold up well under scrutiny. Only a small minority of German Protestants ever thought of themselves as Calvinists.

Historians have not found it easy to agree why Calvinism had the successes it did in Germany. The traditionally accepted view has been that princes who had previously found it impossible to dominate the Church in their territories favoured Calvinism because it held out the prospect of greater central control. This political interpretation has received greater credibility from the fact that the Electors Palatine clearly used the Calvinist cause as a way of enhancing their international standing. However, it has come increasingly under attack from researchers who have been able to show that many of the princes in question were genuinely interested in theological issues, and may well have been motivated primarily by religious motives. The historical debate continues.

Less attempt has been made by historians to account for the failure of Calvinism to make dramatic progress among German-speaking populations. It certainly cannot be explained by arguing that all the Germans who were ripe for conversion to Protestantism had already accepted Lutheranism, for this was clearly not the case. Many nobles in the Habsburg domains became Lutherans long after Calvinism became a competing international phenomenon. Nor was it the case that Lutheranism remained dynamic and expansionist. It is generally accepted that it had mainly lost its energy as a growth movement even before Luther died. So why did Calvinism fail to replace it in the German lands? Could it have been partly because of nationalism? Was Calvinism viewed by Germans as even more of a foreign faith than the Church of Rome? Certainly there was a widespread feeling that Lutheranism was the Protestantism of the Germans. This seems to have been a significant contributory factor in the conversion of many Polish and Hungarian nobles to Calvinism. In areas of central and eastern Europe where Slavs and Germans were intermingled, the Germans tended to have the upper hand. In these countries, to become a Calvinist rather than a Lutheran was to make a public statement of one's racial loyalties. Little research has so far been carried out on the part played by nationalist feelings in supporting or hindering the international spread of Calvinism. When the work is done it may yield some interesting results. Certainly, Calvinism was at its most effective in the French-speaking world.

2 Calvin and France

Whereas German speakers were living in hundreds of different states, spread over a wide geographical area and separated by large populations of other racial groups, the French in the mid-sixteenth century were clearly centred on the territories of the king of France. Within the kingdom of France there were wide variations of language, customs and outlook, but there was a general acceptance that the lawful ruler was the king. There were several great magnates whose influence was paramount in many parts of the kingdom, and thousands of nobles of greater or lesser local importance, but all accepted that, in theory at least, they exercised no sovereignty of their own. The unitary nature of the French state made it very difficult for Protestantism to gain recognition. There either had to be a king who would tolerate religious diversity within his domains, or a king who was himself converted to the faith, or such a collapse of royal authority that states within states effectively came into existence. Certainly it was not possible for Protestantism to make headway as it had in Germany via a patchwork of virtually autonomous city and princely states.

During the first rapidly expansionist period of the Reformation the king of France was Francis I (1515–47). His over-riding concern was his struggle for international supremacy with the Habsburgs, largely in the person of Charles V. He seems to have had no depth of religious faith, although he was a practising Catholic. There was no doubt in his mind that religion should serve the state and not *vice versa*. He made decisions about religious matters according to the political needs of the moment. This resulted in a lack of consistency. Thus the first Frenchmen to be persuaded by Luther's arguments were at times encouraged and at times persecuted, as the young Calvin, among others, found to his cost. One result of the frequent changes of approach was a steady stream of religious exiles (in total numbering tens of thousands) from France. Many were people of substance and education who had committed themselves to the reformed faith when there was little danger in doing so, and who possessed sufficient wealth and worldly wisdom to move to a place of safety when the persecution recommenced.

From the mid-1520s a number of states within Germany openly adopted Lutheranism against the express wishes of the Emperor, Charles V. It was clearly in Francis I's interests to cultivate good relations with their leaders in the hope that they would become his allies in any war with the Habsburgs. This he could best do by adopting a tolerant attitude towards those of his own subjects who had accepted the reformed religion. The political advantage to be gained by favouring Protestantism remained until the end of his reign, but it was constantly counterbalanced by other factors which inclined him towards determined action against heretics within France. The most pressing of these was the intense religious conservatism of two of the country's most influential institutions, the Paris *Parlement* and the Sorbonne (the theological faculty of the University of Paris). It was not that Francis could not act contrary to their wishes: rather that if he did so he was creating political opposition that was best avoided. These internal pressures in favour of religious orthodoxy were at times complemented by external factors. Although Charles V was a strongly committed Catholic, his relations with the Papacy were not always good. Popes tended to play off the Habsburgs against the French whenever possible, in order to provide themselves with room for manoeuvre in the political affairs of Italy. They greatly resented the fact that they were frequently under Charles' domination, and friendship with France offered the possibility of escape from Habsburg tutelage. But whenever Francis wished to take advantage of papal support, it was necessary for him to take stern measures against the Protestants of France.

However, as the persecution of heretics was generally undertaken for the sake of appearances, rather than from a strong sense of conviction, it tended to be conducted in a fairly haphazard manner, normally giving the intended victims plenty of opportunity to escape the consequences of their apostasy. The early escape routes led to the Protestant city-states of Strasbourg and Basle, both of which welcomed religious exiles from France. But neither was French-speaking. Once, towards the end of Francis' reign, Calvin had established a strong enough position in Geneva to suggest that his residence there might be permanent, the advantages offered by the city as a refuge for France's exiles were obvious, and the trickle of 'incomers' rapidly turned into a flood. Yet most of the exiles were unlikely to become permanent residents of the city. Local hostility towards them was never far below the surface, and for many there were restricted opportunities to earn a living once their capital was exhausted. So they tended to shelter until the 'storm' at home blew over. In the process they were exposed to the effects of Calvin's teachings, and many of them became fervent and well-informed supporters. When they returned to their original homes they were able to take with them a clearly understood faith, a good supply of religious literature and knowledge of how to organise themselves effectively. But most of all, they were dedicated to winning further converts within their own communities, which most of them did.

* A political situation within France eventually turned in their favour. Francis I's son, Henry II, was able to maintain the pressure on the Protestants, but his untimely death in 1559 precipitated forty years of civil strife and turmoil during which religious orthodoxy was impossible to maintain. Henry left a widow and a young family. His widow, Catherine de Medici, was a remarkable woman of great energy, great resilience and considerable (if inconsistent) political skill. She was the power behind the throne for the next fifteen years as three of her somewhat inadequate sons became king one after the other. But, although she was able to salvage some of the monarchy's powers, she was never able to dominate the situation. As a woman and a foreigner, with a claim to rule based on motherhood rather than birth, she could not resist the demands of the country's great magnates to be allowed to

wield effective power. It was the lengthy struggle between an enfeebled monarchy and competing noble factions that presented Protestantism with its great opportunity.

It was not merely that the Protestants took advantage of the lack of strong national leadership to maintain their position. They gained from the fact that one of the two factions struggling for power chose to identify itself totally with the Protestant cause. The supporters of this faction were known as Huguenots (probably a corruption of the name of one of the Genevan factions of the mid-1530s), and the term was applied to all Protestants in France from about 1560 onwards. The first leaders of the Huguenot faction were Bourbons and Chatillons, members of two of the most powerful families in France. Through the system of clientage, by which magnates built up support in the regions by offering patronage to local families of importance, the Huguenots rapidly gained effective control of much of southern, western and central France. Even Normandy was largely under their control until the First Civil War of 1562–63. They were therefore able to ensure the protection of Protestants in the areas which were dominated by their clients. They also expected that their supporters would become members of the Reformed Churches that were being established in the majority of French towns and cities (but not in the countryside). As a consequence, the number of nominal Protestants in France grew very rapidly during the early 1560s, when it seemed that Calvinism might sweep all before it.

Historians have long disputed the extent to which the conversions were a result of genuine religious conviction as opposed to mere political expediency. No clear consensus has emerged, which is hardly surprising given the nature of the dispute and of the available evidence. It is difficult enough for the individual to be certain of his or her own motivation in a particular situation. It is even harder for the historian to reach convincing conclusions about the motivation of people from the past; and it is virtually impossible to identify with any degree of certainty the collective motivation of a group of historical characters about whom little direct evidence exists. What is fairly certain is that some leading Huguenots were guided largely by religious principles, while others were certainly not. But it would be dangerous to generalise from the available evidence, or to allow the desire to produce a straightforward answer (especially one to coincide with one's own prejudices) to lead to suggestions of greater certainty than is possible. So, while general statements about the range of motivation seemingly exhibited by the Huguenot leadership are defensible, it would be unreasonable to do more than speculate about what might have been the balance between the various motivations.

* However, there seems little doubt that Admiral Coligny, a member of the Chatillon branch of the Montmorency family and the most prominent Huguenot of the 1560s, was a genuine follower of Calvin. In

fact, he was probably the most ardent Calvinist ever to secure major political influence in France, and for a time it even seemed possible that he would convert the young king, Charles IX (1560–74), to total sympathy for his cause. But the Huguenots' hopes were shattered in 1572, just at the moment when it seemed certain that an alliance was to be cemented between France and the opponents of Philip II in the Netherlands, aimed at initiating some sort of Protestant crusade against the Catholic king of Spain. Historians disagree about what probably happened, but it seems likely that Catherine de Medici panicked. She believed that the Huguenots were about to seize control of the country, and in order to prevent this she agreed to the assassination of Coligny. When the attempt failed, she feared that the details of the plot would soon become widely known. In a desperate attempt to protect herself from vengeance she authorised the killing of the leading Huguenots, who were gathered in Paris to celebrate the marriage of one of their leaders. The Paris militia, joined by the mob, carried out their instructions with excessive zeal and the result was the St Bartholomew's Day Massacre in which thousands (no exact count was made) of Huguenots, including Coligny and many of the other leaders, were hunted down and hacked to death in the houses and streets of Paris. The killings were copied in twelve other towns and cities.

The Massacre completely altered the balance of political power in France. As the Huguenots' position had been dramatically weakened, it was no longer possible for the monarchy to play off one faction against the other. So control passed into the hands of the Guise faction, which was as committed to the maintenance of Catholic domination as the Huguenots were to the protection of Protestantism. Persecution of Calvinists recommenced with vigour, and with great speed hundreds of Huguenot nobles reasserted their allegiance to the Catholic Church. This, of course, has led historians to conclude that they were not sincere Protestants, and that they had become Calvinists merely as a political expedient. There is clear evidence that this was so in a number of cases, but it would be unwise to generalise from this – apart from drawing the obvious conclusion that many Huguenots were not prepared to die for their faith. Certainly, it is not possible to estimate with any degree of accuracy just how many of the Huguenot nobles were *politiques* (people who used religion for political purposes).

* From 1572 to 1589, the Huguenots were faced with the choice between rebellion, death and abandoning their faith. Few were prepared to choose death. In the late 1550s Calvin had already modified his teachings on the right to resist tyrants (see page 65), and after his death in 1564 his successor, Beza, along with other leading second-generation Calvinists, further developed justifications for rebellion. Their argument was based on the premise that God had not granted power to kings unconditionally. They maintained that He had granted power to lower-order magistrates (office holders in the regions and

localities) so that they could lead resistance to tyrants, even going to the lengths of deposing them if necessary. This justification of 'aristocratic rebellion', of course, fell far short of supporting the democratic ideal that power should lie with the people. However, there were some Calvinists who went that far. They were rapidly disowned by the Church establishment, which was only prepared to support publications such as that by the Huguenot nobleman, Philippe du Plessis-Mornay. His book, *Vindiciae contra Tyrannos*, which appeared in 1579 and encapsulated the 'aristocratic' argument, rapidly became the standard Calvinist work on the subject.

So the Huguenots were well-equipped with a theoretical justification for continuing their struggle to gain power in France. The Wars of Religion, which had started in 1562, therefore continued. But neither side was able to gain total dominance, even with the active help of their co-religionists abroad, and the fighting drifted on from inconclusive truce to inconclusive truce. The pattern was interrupted by the death of Henry II's last remaining son, Henry III, in 1589. There was no member of his family to follow him, and the succession passed to Henry of Navarre, a distant relative. As chance would have it, Henry was a Bourbon, a Protestant and the leader of the Huguenot cause. Overnight the rebels became the supporters of the rightful king!

Henry IV knew that warfare could not resolve the situation, as neither side was strong enough to secure outright victory. He therefore sought to bring peace to his exhausted country by political action. In return for the support of many of the leading Catholics, he changed his religion and became a Catholic himself. He could not overcome the outrage of the Huguenots at this desertion, but he was able to end their active opposition by assuring them of toleration through the terms of the Edict of Nantes in 1598. This Edict stipulated where Huguenots would have the right to worship and outlawed discrimination against them in educational and political matters. It was to provide the framework for religious peace in France for most of the seventeenth century.

Historical opinion has generally regarded the Edict of Nantes as the beginning of the end of Calvinism in France. Perhaps there has been a large amount of historical hindsight in this judgement. Authors have been aware that not only did the Huguenots fail to gain more ground during their century of toleration, but that they were actually forced to abandon either their faith or their country when Louis XIV revoked the Edict in 1685. The argument has been that the true significance of the Edict was not that it protected the Protestant position, but that it guaranteed the survival of Catholicism in all parts of France while making it impossible for Calvinism to spread into areas in which it had been weak in 1598. This interpretation is attractive but has weaknesses in that it seems to depend upon the assumption that people were only converted to Calvinism when the law of the land allowed it. This was patently not so, and had Calvinism been a dynamic force in seventeenth century France no Edict would have prevented its expansion.

More convincing is an argument that suggests that the Edict of Nantes signalled (but in no way caused) the failure of Calvinism to establish control in France. As a religion of extremists, it was never likely to appeal to more than a minority in any community. History seems to show that extremism is only ever successful if its supporters gain control of the organs of government and impose their solutions on a population that is, at worst, generally acquiescent. France was too large and diverse for this to happen, as Henry of Navarre realised only too well. No sixteenth century king of France was powerful enough to be able to change the religious affiliations of the large majority of his subjects. Calvinism could only have gained control in France if, under the stress of prolonged civil war, the country had broken up into a number of semi-independent states as existed in Germany or Switzerland. There was no realistic possibility that it would gain control of one of the largest and richest states of Europe.

* It would therefore be unfair to suggest that Calvinism was a failure in France. It would be more appropriate to explore the extent and reasons for what was undoubtedly its success. The fact that about ten percent of the population (nearly all town dwellers who were not poor) were practising Calvinists by 1600 may seem to suggest very limited penetration, but this actually represented about two million men, women and children who, in generally adverse conditions, had decided to follow the reformed faith. Of course, many of them were undoubtedly *politiques* who became nominal Calvinists largely because it appeared to be to their advantage socially or politically. But there were certainly hundreds of thousands of people who took their commitment seriously. This was a number many times larger than the size of Calvin's own Church in Geneva, and constituted a major extension of the reformer's sphere of influence. It was one of the greatest triumphs that Calvinism was to achieve as a faith of popular acclaim.

There is no simple explanation for this. Many of the reasons must be sought in the political situation within the country, especially from 1559 onwards when the removal of a strong central authority opened the way for the eruption of factional feuding. The fact that one of the two major groupings adopted Calvinism as one of its causes meant that many people who would otherwise have remained Catholics decided to throw in their lot with the reformed Church. It also meant that small groups of committed Calvinists within many communities were afforded protection that they would not have received in normal times. But it would be a mistake to take this argument too far, as recent trends in historical interpretation have been in danger of doing by overstressing the political reasons for the Calvinists' success in France. It is true that for more than thirty years the political situation was particularly

'No other religious seer did more for France/Nor was Scotland so enriched by any other prophet'

favourable to the spread of Protestantism, but situations have to be taken advantage of. The Huguenots' success was in no sense automatic. Converts had to be won.

During the last ten years of his life, through a period of seriously declining health, Calvin spent more time worrying about the situation in France than about anything else. He agonised over his teachings on the right to resist, he grieved over the fate of those of his missionaries who were captured and killed, he gave concentrated attention to the preparation of ministers returning to his native country, and he devoted great care to wooing those important nobles whose conversion was likely to lead to the creation of major followings among their supporters. It is not known exactly how many journeys into France were undertaken by preachers from Geneva, but the figure certainly ran into many hundreds. Nor is it known how many copies of Calvin's writings were printed in Geneva and smuggled into France, or how many requests for advice and guidance were answered, often in Calvin's own hand. But what is known is that Catholic leaders were in no doubt that their problems stemmed from Geneva, and it became common usage to describe the Wars of Religion as a struggle between Geneva and Rome. Certainly, French Calvinists in triumph or adversity were greatly encouraged by the existence of a secure 'headquarters' abroad.

It has frequently been said that the Calvinists' two great advantages over other contemporary forms of Christianity were organisation and discipline. This certainly seems to have been the case in France. It would have been very easy for the first small groups of Calvinists in any district to have become isolated and dispirited, especially when they were denied any form of official approval. But because of the form of Church organisation all Calvinists were expected to adopt, and because of the mutual support that was available to all members, considerable strength was acquired by even small groups. This strength was greatly and rapidly enhanced by the way in which the early Huguenots extended Calvin's thinking on Church organisation from a system which suited a small city-state with its twenty satellite villages to one which was appropriate for a large and populous nation state. Within a short time local churches were organised into district and provincial synods, and in 1559 the first national synod was held in Paris. It was therefore possible for the Calvinists in France to act in a co-ordinated manner throughout the period of the civil wars, both in their mutual defence and in planning and conducting offensive measures. It took some time for the Catholics to organise themselves in a similarly effective fashion.

It is also clear that the simplicity and coherence of Calvin's teachings were a large part of their appeal to those who had previously encountered Protestantism only in the form of Lutheranism. Calvin, like Luther, unashamedly produced publications that were aimed at the relatively unsophisticated lay audiences of his time. But whereas Luther tended to appeal to the emotions, especially those associated with a sense of German national identity, Calvin sought to convince by reason. This was particularly appropriate in the case of the French nobility which was renowned for its worldly wisdom. It has been estimated that half of their number became converts between 1555 and 1562. The process was made easier by the fact that Calvin consciously avoided confusing complications in writing for such an audience. When attacked for the theological unsoundness of some of the arguments used in these writings, he was quite prepared to defend himself by explaining that he had only intended this work to be read by lay people!

How much of Calvinism's (as opposed to Lutheranism's) success in France is explicable in terms of national sentiment is not known. Certainly there is no evidence of Luther's ideas being rejected in France because they were 'foreign', although there is a suspicion that Calvin was particularly prized by many French people because he was in a special sense 'theirs'. Such sentiment is rarely quantifiable, but it is no less real because of that. France was Calvinism's 'natural' missionary territory, and it was remarkably successful in gaining ground there, even if the size of the task was eventually to be beyond its capabilities.

3 The Netherlands

If the initial successes of Calvinism in France can be regarded as representing ultimately unfulfilled potential, the same cannot be said of the Netherlands. By the early seventeenth century the United Provinces (Holland) was an officially Calvinist state in which no other form of religion was tolerated. Historians have been very keen to establish the reasons for this difference between France and the Netherlands in the degree of Calvinism's long-term success. They have generally sought explanations that concentrate on the ways in which the political situations in the two countries differed.

During the second half of the sixteenth century the northern provinces of the Netherlands were able to establish a *de facto* independent state, the United Provinces, by breaking free from the control of their rightful ruler, the king of Spain. Yet this 'Revolt of the Netherlands' was not successful in the southern provinces, in which the king regained control – a control that was maintained by the Habsburg family until the late eighteenth century. In these southern provinces the Catholic Church retained its dominant position and pockets of Calvinism were gradually eradicated, as they were in France. There therefore seems to be a clear correlation between the success of rebellion and the success of Calvinism.

The link between the two appears even stronger when it is realised that Calvinism was initially much more firmly established in the southern Netherlands than in the province that were successful in breaking free from Spain. This early success in the south was not at all surprising. The people were predominantly French-speaking and were therefore open to influences that spread across their southern frontier. The area contained some of the largest and most industrially advanced cities in Europe, with populations that were generally interested in new ideas and were not afraid to adopt them; and the resistance to what was regarded as Spanish oppression was initially most widespread there.

Yet Calvinism eventually disappeared in the south, while it carried all before it in the more backward north. The only reasonable explanation for this disparity appears to be that the two areas experienced opposite political fates.

* Until relatively recent times, the orthodox view about religion and the revolt of the Netherlands was that the revolt was successful largely because it was a rebellion of Calvinist subjects against a Catholic lord. It was assumed that Calvinism was the cause and that success was the effect. This interpretation has been challenged so successfully that it is no longer credible. It has been shown that in many parts of the north, the Calvinists were a tiny and insignificant minority at the time rebel control was established; that the leading aristocratic rebels, especially William of Orange, were *politiques* who adopted Calvinism because it helped to create a distance between themselves and their Spanish rulers; and that popular support for the rebellion was not only variable and unreliable, but was motivated much more by economic than religious factors. Certainly, it is no longer possible to maintain convincingly that Calvinism was a major cause of the success of the Dutch Revolt.

In fact, it is now increasingly clear that Calvinism was one of the main reasons why the Revolt was not successful in the southern Netherlands. At times in the 1570s it seemed that an effectively independent state of the Netherlands would be created whose boundaries would coincide with those of the Spanish possessions. But this promising position was lost to the rebels who had gradually to accept that at least half of the country would remain under Spanish control. This situation arose largely because the social *élites* of the southern Netherlands, the territorial magnates and the leading merchants and industrialists of the towns and cities, found the prospect of re-imposed Spanish rule less frightening than the possibility of a social revolution which they feared would follow the creation of an independent state. Their fears had been awoken by the actions and attitudes of Calvinist extremists within the region. These were predominantly drawn from the ranks of the artisans, the skilled workers who were allowed to play no direct part in their own government. For centuries they had been in periodic violent dispute with their social superiors who largely controlled their economic fate. They made it clear that they would use the disciplinary powers of the Church, once Calvinism was exclusively established, to remove the predominant influence of the ruling oligarchies. When in 1577–78 this happened in southern city after southern city, starting with Brussels and Ghent, any hope of the Revolt gaining united support in the region disappeared. It took seven or eight years for the forces of reaction to build up sufficient military strength to reconquer the cities, but once this was done the elimination of Calvinism in the districts under Spanish control was well under way.

Why then was Calvinism able to both gain and retain control in the north? There can be no certainty, but the answer seems to be that the official support given to the early converts allowed them to flourish and to win further recruits when they were at their most vulnerable. It also meant that the Reformed Churches were established under the auspices of, and largely under the control of, the existing authorities, and were therefore not seen as a threat to the prevailing power structure. This was in marked contrast to what happened in the south, and was a vital distinction.

Yet it does not explain why the small number of Calvinists in the north were able to win for their Church the status of the sole recognised form of religion. Why were they able to over-ride the wishes of the Catholic majority? It was certainly not the wish of William of Orange and the other political leaders of the Revolt that this should happen, for their constant negotiating position with the representatives of Philip II was that they merely sought religious toleration. But the refusal of the Spanish to contemplate anything but exclusive rights of worship for the Catholics left the rebel leadership with little alternative but to give way to the Calvinists who claimed similar exclusive rights for themselves. The pressure to do this was particularly strong given the fact that the Calvinists were one of the few groups to give complete and unfailing support to the rebel cause. If William of Orange had lost their active support he might have found the Revolt crumbling completely. He was not prepared to risk this. But even with a very high level of official support, and with the large scale influx of co-religionist refugees from the south, it still took Calvinism more than a generation to become the religion of the majority within any of the territories of the United Provinces. In some districts it never attracted more than a small minority of the population, despite its status as the only officially recognised Church. This is not surprising, for many countries (as opposed to city-states) that adopted the Reformation experienced similar difficulties in converting the masses. These facts certainly reinforce the argument that without official support Protestantism stood little chance of establishing itself anywhere on a permanent basis.

* What happened in the Netherlands illustrates well the differences between the three major strands of Protestantism – Lutheranism, Anabaptism and Calvinism. Lutheranism won numbers of converts, especially among the highly educated, during the 1520s, but was unable to make real headway in the face of determined opposition from the ruler, Charles V. Its sympathisers were forced either to recant, to flee or to suffer death for their beliefs. Even Erasmus (hardly a Lutheran, but suspected of reformist tendencies) decided that it would be safer to transfer his residence to Switzerland. In the 1520s and 1530s, the Anabaptists secured a lasting foothold among the lower orders in many of the towns where they were able to survive without coming into official view. But because they lacked organisation and structure they

were totally dependent on the charisma of individual leaders, and their fortunes seem to have ebbed and flowed accordingly. They never became more than a somewhat subversive minority underground movement. Calvinism, on the other hand, became the state religion of the United Provinces, taking over many Anabaptist communities as it did so. Because it possessed a coherent and readily understood set of beliefs, and was organised in such a way that it was able both to defend itself and to reach out for fresh converts, it was well prepared to take advantage of the political uncertainties that were caused by the opposition of Philip II's style of government. In the process, it further earned for itself the reputation of being the religion of revolution.

4 Scotland

The potentially revolutionary nature of Calvinism was first, and most convincingly, demonstrated in Scotland. In 1559–60, even before the outbreak of the Wars of Religion in France and the religious unrest in the Netherlands, a successful Calvinist Reformation involving the seizure of effective political power had taken place there. Such was the extent and savagery of the violence which accompanied the changes that uncommitted as well as Catholic opinion in Europe was tempted to conclude that Geneva was the source of a great and dangerous social and political evil. Thereafter it was difficult for Calvinism to disassociate itself in Catholic countries from the charge that it was an underminer of political stability and civilised values.

Yet it would be patently unfair to blame Calvin or the Church of Geneva for what happened in Scotland. Events there were totally outside their control, and were dictated by the interaction of the local political situation and the personalities and values of the leading figures involved. In the sixteenth century most continental Europeans, if they had heard of it at all, regarded this small and poor northern independent kingdom as lying right at the edge of (and possibly beyond) the civilised world. There was a ready assumption that nothing good could happen there. Elements of the prevailing culture substantiated this view. Political activity, which was dominated by the fifty or so nobles, was characterised by treachery, deceit and the speedy resort to violence. The coldblooded murder of opponents was so much the norm – not the exception as in the more prosperous countries of Europe – that it was unusual for a politically active person to die of natural causes. The Church was particularly corrupt, even by the low standards of the time. Senior positions were virtually monopolised by the bastards of the Crown and the younger sons of the leading families, who used the Church merely as a convenient source of income. Little spiritual comfort was available to people from the poorly prepared curates who generally served in the parishes in place of the absentee priests.

During the 1520s and 1530s, Lutheran ideas found some support, especially around the ports in the east of the country which regularly conducted trade with Germany. But the authorities had little difficulty in preventing the development of any widespread popular sympathy for the idea of Church reform. The occasional burning of heretics was a sufficient deterrent. The situation changed dramatically in the years after 1542 when the king, James V, died, leaving as his successor his baby daughter, Mary Queen of Scots. The long minority that followed gave ample scope for more than the usual amount of factional feuding as efforts were made to advance individual interests at the expense of the weakened monarchy.

Matters were complicated by the international dimension to the contest. France and England had been traditional enemies for centuries. French kings throughout this time had tended to use Scotland as a way of discomfitting the English, especially by encouraging the Scots to mount raids into England as a distraction. This led to there being constant competition between England and France for political influence in Edinburgh. France was normally successful, as suggested by the fact that James V had married into an prominent French family, the Guises, rather than seeking dynastic links in England. When he died, his widow, Mary of Guise (often known as Mary of Lorraine), gradually established a position of political dominance in Scotland. She relied on French money and French troops in doing so. Her influence was used both to further French interests and to protect the position of the Catholic Church. A marriage was arranged between her daughter and Francis, the heir to the French throne, in the expectation that Scotland would thereby become a French possession. But she was less successful in her dealings with the Protestants, whose power and influence extended rapidly under the protection of a number of nobles who saw that religion could be used as a weapon in their feuding. To make matters worse, the English (except during the reign of Mary I between 1553 and 1558) encouraged the growth of a Protestant party in Scotland both by giving money to potentially key supporters and by promising future assistance.

By 1559 the threat to continued Scottish independence appeared to be great. Mary Queen of Scots was living permanently abroad with her husband, who had just become king of France. Scottish policy seemed to be decided by Mary of Guise with French interests only in mind – which was hardly surprising as all her advisers were foreigners. It seemed that it would not be long before King Francis II of France would be declared King Francis I of Scotland. In this situation the self-seeking nobles who wished to acquire Mary's political power for themselves were able to represent themselves as national saviours who were rescuing the country from both political and religious domination from abroad. They capitalised on anti-foreign as well as pro-Protestant feelings. In a civil war that lasted less than two years, they were able to drive out the French, assisted by the death of Mary of Guise, and to establish themselves in power as the Queen's representatives. In the process they ushered in a Calvinist reformation.

Few of the nobles who brought about this transformation seem to have had any great interest in religion. Most of them became nominal Protestants for reasons of political expediency. But there were many people at the social level below them who were strongly committed to the Calvinist cause. In the countryside these were the lairds, the landowning gentry, and in the towns the burgesses, the merchants and traders who exercised political control. However, they were a small minority of the total population and they were not sufficiently powerful to impose their wishes on the nation as a whole. They needed the active support of their social superiors. Had this not been gained and retained, it is probable that the Reformation in Scotland would have been similar to the Reformation in England where, under both Henry VIII and Elizabeth I, political considerations were paramount. But this was not the case in Scotland, largely because of the activities of one man – John Knox.

* Knox probably had the greatest effect on subsequent history of any follower of Calvin. He was a remarkable man. Today he would be described as 'larger than life'. Even in his own time, when extraordinary characters seemed to abound, he was unusual. His impact was almost totally achieved by force of personality. He dominated most of those around him with his highly aggressive statements of certainty against which it was difficult to argue. Issues were all black or all white: qualifying words were rarely used. He came to regard himself as God's mouthpiece for his country, pre-ordained to make His wishes known to the people, and to insist that they were carried out. He was no respecter of persons and was daunted by few situations. This arose partly from his own natural arrogance, which had always made it difficult for him to accept control or correction from anyone, and partly from his total conviction that God was directing all his actions and that his fate was already sealed. There were obvious parallels with Calvin's approach to his work in Geneva, but there were also very distinct differences. Whereas Calvin was genuinely a reluctant holder of the centre stage, Knox thirsted for fame and status. He lacked the calm temperament and logical mind which enabled Calvin in most situations to assess what was realistically achievable and to act accordingly. Some of his biographers have attempted to prove that he was a shrewd politician, but they have done no more than show that at times he seems to have acted with an awareness of political implications. More frequently, however, especially as he grew older, his actions were dictated by his hot temper and his deep-seated angers and hatreds. People were either captivated by him or were passionately opposed to him. It was not possible to ignore him.

In normal times the 'system' would have kept him down, and for much of his life it did. It took him more than forty years to achieve prominence. Much is unclear about this period of his life, as is only to be expected of somebody whose rise from fairly humble origins (his father was a not very prosperous merchant) was slow and uncertain. The situation is not helped by the fact that much of our evidence comes from Knox's own writings, and is frequently unreliable. It was not that Knox's memory was bad but that his working definition of truth was unconventional. He seems genuinely to have believed that any statement was true as long as it furthered God's work. He was therefore sincere in his denunciation of others for lying, even when he needed to alter or even invent facts to substantiate his allegations. Typical of the uncertainty are the doubts that surround the year of his birth. For centuries it has been believed that he was born in 1505, but it now appears almost certain that the correct date was 1514. However, there is no doubt that he became a Catholic priest and greatly resented the fact that his lack of social contacts precluded his advancement, despite his obvious and clearly demonstrated talents.

His conversion to Protestantism was the result of his own reading of the Bible, coupled with exposure to the influence of evangelical preachers. It had nothing to do with Calvin, whose impact on him came later, when Knox was a religious refugee searching for a sympathetic temporary home on the continent. The aggressively Catholic regimes of Mary of Guise in Scotland and Mary I in England meant that there was no welcome for him anywhere in Britain. His faith was already tried and tested by the time he found his way to Geneva for the first time in 1554, for he had had to survive nineteen months as a galley slave in France. He had been subjected to this punishment following his capture by Mary of Guise's French troops. The punishment was so severe because he had been arrested along with a group of Protestant rebels who had assassinated the Archbishop of St Andrews, the Primate of the Catholic Church in Scotland, in 1546. The rebels had exacerbated their crime by seizing the castle of St Andrews and holding it for more than a year, despite all the government's efforts to unseat them. Knox had joined them part-way through their occupation of the castle.

★ On his arrival in Geneva, Knox was immediately attracted by Calvinism. Presumably he readily sympathised with both its certainty and its emphasis on discipline. But he was no slavish disciple. He took from Calvin's teachings what fitted into his own views, while conveniently ignoring what did not. This was nowhere more clearly demonstrated than in his writings on the obedience owed to monarchs. In 1558 he published anonymously and secretly in Geneva his *The First Blast of the Trumpet against the Monstrous Regiment of Women* (regiment means government). He knew that Calvin would greatly disapprove of it, but he went ahead with it nonetheless. His motives in writing the pamphlet are obscure, but there is no doubting its impact. It rapidly became notorious in religious and political circles throughout Europe, where it attracted general criticism and little support. It did more than any other single thing to forge the link in people's minds between Calvinism and revolution. It argued the extreme case that it was unnatural and against God's wishes for women to rule. It was primarily targeted at Mary I of England who was a Catholic and Knox's arch enemy, but it included some hostile comments on women in general. This was in conformity with the common male prejudices of the time, in contrast with its call to Mary's subjects to rise up and overthrow her, which scandalised Catholic and Protestant opinion alike.

1 First, they ought to remove from honour and authority that monster in nature; so call I a woman clad in the habit of a man, yea, a woman against nature reigning above man. Secondly, if any presume to defend that impiety, they ought not fear first to
5 pronounce, and then after to execute against them, the sentence of death.

Knox followed up *The First Blast* with a series of pamphlets aimed specifically at Scotland. In them he developed his views further.

1 Now the common song of all men is, 'We must obey our kings, be they good or be they bad; for God has so commanded'. But horrible shall the vengeance be that shall be poured forth upon such blasphemers of God's holy name and ordinance . . . True it
5 is, God hath commanded kings to be obeyed, but like true it is, that in things which they commit against His glory, or when cruelly without cause they rage against their brethren, the members of Christ's body, He hath commanded no obedience, but rather He hath approved, yea, and greatly rewarded such as
10 have opposed themselves to their ungodly commandments and blind rage.

He summarised his position in four propositions:

1 1. It is not birth only, nor propinquity of blood, that maketh a king lawfully to reign above a people professing Christ Jesus and His eternal verity, but in his election must the ordinance which God hath established in the election of inferior judges
5 be observed.
2. No manifest idolater nor notorious transgressor of God's holy precepts ought to be promoted to any public regiment, honour or dignity in any realm, province or city that has subjected the self to Christ Jesus and His blessed Evangel.
10 3. Neither can oath nor promise bind any such people to obey and maintain tyrants against God and against His truth known.
4. But if rashly they have promoted any manifest wicked person, or yet ignorantly have chosen such a one as after declareth
15 himself unworthy of regiment above the people of God (and

such be all idolaters and cruel persecutors) most justly may the same men depose and punish him that unadvisedly before they did nominate, appoint and elect.

Knox's writings resulted in him becoming one of the most hated men of his time in almost all ruling circles. It also seriously damaged Geneva's standing abroad. Calvin attempted to disassociate himself from the views of his Scottish follower, but in England he was especially unsuccessful. Elizabeth I, who ascended the throne only a few months after the appearance of *The First Blast*, was unprepared to accept assurances that it in no way reflected the official Calvinist position. In Scotland, however, Knox's teachings were eagerly welcomed by those nobles who sought a convincing justification for the overthrow of Mary of Guise as regent in her daughter's absence. This helped to establish Knox's position as one of Scotland's most influential Protestant churchmen. He increased his influence further during the political turmoil of the 1560s, although he had lost his central importance by the time of his death in 1572.

*   The Protestant Church in Scotland was highly organised. In its early years it was in many ways a state within a state. From late 1557 onwards, members were expected to make a covenant with the Congregation (the name the Protestants used to describe themselves) promising to come to the aid of any 'brother' who was in danger because of his faith. The fact that this system worked in practice made it very difficult for official action to be taken against Protestants. Whenever it was attempted, the rapid appearance of armed bands of protesters, normally led by one or more of the Lords of the Congregation, made it impossible to proceed. This willingness to engage in concerted action continued once the Reformation was legally adopted by the Scottish parliament in 1560 and the celebration of the Mass was outlawed. This ability to take defensive action as necessary was important because, from August 1561 to July 1567, Scotland was in the unique position of being a Protestant state ruled over by a Catholic monarch. Mary's time as Queen of France had been cut short by the death of her young husband in 1560, before she could produce an heir to their joint thrones, and she had reluctantly returned to her native land to perform her duties as sovereign. There was naturally a suspicion among the Protestants that, although she had promised to respect the religious settlement that had been made in her absence, Mary would seek every opportunity to turn the tables on them. This was reinforced by Mary's refusal to return unless it was agreed that the Mass could be celebrated in her presence.

*   Knox attempted to provide the Scottish Church with a Genevan style of organisation. He was successful in establishing the Church's control over its beliefs, the selection of ministers and the use of

Nineteenth century illustration of John Knox preaching in Edinburgh in 1559

excommunication, while an impressive structure of self-government, based on local and national Church Sessions or Assemblies (the equivalent of synods), was set up, ensuring that the government would find it virtually impossible to establish political control of the Church. However, Knox's efforts to reverse the situation and bring the government essentially under the Church's control were effectively resisted by friend and foe alike among the ruling group of monarch and nobles. They were determined to protect their traditional status as being effectively above the law. They had no intention of allowing their conduct to be constrained by the dictates of low-born churchmen.

Knox's reaction to this was inconsistent. Sometimes, apparently having accepted the realities of political power, he offered support to Protestant lords whose life-styles seemed to mark them out as reprobates: at other times he attacked the Queen so violently in his sermons that he clearly laid himself open to charges of treason. But neither approach led to effective legal sanctions being imposed on those who failed to accept the Church's discipline. There had to be reliance on the force of social pressure. This was very effective among the population at large, but was largely ignored by those who regarded themselves as being socially superior. By the mid-1560s Knox's frequent rantings against Mary from the pulpit of St Giles Cathedral in Edinburgh had turned him into an object of embarrassment for most of the Protestant lords. It is probable that the Queen could have silenced him permanently if she had shown more determination or political good sense. As it was, she destroyed her position by allowing himself to become implicated in the murder of her second husband in 1566 and by then choosing his presumed murderer as her third husband. She was forced to abdicate in 1567.

Knox's thinking on the structure and organisation of the Church was explained in *The Book of Discipline*. This was drawn up by Knox and his leading colleagues in 1560. It was given the partial force of law in 1561, although it was never properly confirmed, and was only put into effect in as far as it suited the purposes of the ruling group of the time. It dealt with the procedures for the election of ministers and for their payment. It also established a system of superintendents to replace bishops, and laid down that they should spend all their time touring their districts and supervising the work of the ministers. This part of *The Book of Discipline* was speedily implemented, but other sections were not. In particular, the clauses stipulating that all children should attend school were not put into effect for over a century, although both their initial inclusion and their eventual introduction provide evidence that formal education was more highly valued in Scotland than in most other parts of the world.

Most of the regulations followed Calvin's Genevan model fairly closely, with modifications to suit the particular circumstances of Scotland and Knox's rather more punitive mentality. Or some issues

Knox sought Calvin's specific advice, but ignored it if it did not fit in with his existing views. When his opinion was asked, Calvin replied that the Church should be prepared to baptise the children of excommunicated people. *The Book of Discipline* stated that

1 His [the excommunicated person's] children, begotten or born after that sentence and before his repentance, may not be admitted to baptism until either they be of age to require the same, or else the mother, or some of his especial friends,
5 members of the Church, offer and present the child, abhorring and condemning the iniquity and obstinate contempt of the impenitent. If any think it severe that the child should be punished for the iniquity of the father, let them understand that the sacraments appertain only to the faithful and to their seed.
10 Such as stubbornly contemn all Godly admonition and obstinately remain to their iniquity cannot be accounted amongst the faithful.

Yet it would be misleading to stress the differences between Calvin and his Scottish followers. They were in agreement on almost all essentials, and in matters of discipline their shared purpose was primarily to secure sinners' repentance. Neither advocated the use of excommunication except in extreme cases where every effort to bring about a change in behaviour had failed, and both showed considerable patience in the face of initial rejections. The differences that existed were partly caused by the differing circumstances in Scotland and Geneva, and partly resulted from the personalities and prejudices of the two men. Knox was never able to establish the degree of control over daily life in Scotland that Calvin managed during the last years of his life in Geneva, largely because the monarch and the nobles were beyond the power of the people. Nor was he able to overcome what became almost his paranoia about women. His hatred of Mary Queen of Scots led him to adopt indefensible positions. He was even prepared to countenance political murders if they damaged Mary's position. In his dealings with his monarch he was clearly shown at his worst. But his failings do not detract from the impact he had on the history of his country. Had it not been for his powerful advocacy of Calvinist doctrine and forms of organisation, there is little doubt that at some point in the 1560s the Protestant nobles would have been prepared to modify the Reformation settlement in Scotland to bring it into line with the situation in England, as the price to be paid for obtaining support from south of the border. Knox made it impossible for this to happen. His stance secured Calvinism the opportunity to consolidate its position. Although the process had hardly begun in many parts of the country by the time he died, it was subsequently to shape the values and attitudes of Scottish society for nearly four hundred years.

5 England and America

Calvinism would possibly have had a greater impact on England had it not been for the work of Knox. Certainly the prospects were very good up to 1558 when *The First Blast* was published. Not that they had always been so. Until 1547, when Henry VIII died, 'extreme' Protestants had found it safer to live outside the country than within. But the reign of Edward VI (1547–53) had given English Calvinists every encouragement, and it had seemed possible at the time that England would become the first Calvinist nation state. The young king was known to be sympathetic, his most powerful nobles were supporters, and the monarchy was powerful enough to impose its will in religious matters in most parts of the country. However, the untimely death of the king and the accession of his Catholic sister, Mary, was an important setback, although it was expected to be only temporary. Most of the religious refugees who fled to the Rhineland and the Swiss cities, including Geneva, did not expect to be away from their country for many years. They were confident that God would not allow Mary to live for longer than was necessary to punish England for its recent sins. They knew that when she died the new monarch would be her sister, Elizabeth, who was known to be a Protestant at heart.

It seems certain that when Elizabeth became Queen of England in 1558 her attitude towards Calvinism was coloured by the writings of Knox. Calvin tried to undo the damage, but it was too late for his letters to have any chance of changing her mind. Elizabeth had decided that Calvinism was a creed which brought civil war in its train, and she was determined to do all in her power to avoid inter-communal strife in her kingdom. She was also determined that she would have as few dealings as possible with those who encouraged and sided with rebellion against lawful rulers. She retained elements of this determination even when it was against her interests to do so. It would, for instance, have been to England's advantage had she supported the Dutch in their revolt against Philip II earlier than she did. There was therefore little possibility that she would be prepared to allow the Church of England to become Calvinist in its structure or organisation. She was in no doubt that she must retain political control of the Church if civil war was to be avoided. However, she was unlikely to take action against individual Calvinists for their beliefs as long as they were prepared to accept the religious settlement that she had made. As a result, the number of Calvinists (often known as Puritans) within the country steadily grew, but they were unable to organise themselves in the way that their co-religionists in Scotland, France and the Netherlands were doing. Elizabeth was shrewd enough to realise that by taking no action against them, except when their intolerance of others could not be kept within bounds, she was avoiding the situation in which they would feel that they must fight for their faith. Thus England avoided, for the time being at least, the Wars of Religion that were afflicting most of northern Europe.

It was of no real concern to Elizabeth that, in the process, the theology of her Church was considerably affected by Calvin's teachings. Her interest was primarily in political, not religious, affairs. So, by the time of the Queen's death in 1603, the Church of England was an uneasy mixture of Catholicism and Protestantism. Its structure and organisation were little altered from pre-Reformation days, except that the monarch rather than the Pope was Head of the Church. Its services looked and sounded very similar to their Catholic counterparts. Its teachings, however, were very different. The majority of Calvin's distinctive theological interpretations were widely accepted, although it would be an exaggeration to describe the Elizabethan Church as essentially Calvinist. Many theologians had contributed to the rich mixture of beliefs that was current in England. Heindrich Bullinger exercised great influence from Zurich, which resulted in Zwinglian traditions being firmly entrenched in the Church of England. But perhaps the most significant contributor to late sixteenth century theological thinking in England was an Italian, known in English as Peter Martyr, whose book *Common Places* was much more widely read than was Calvin's *Institutio*. So it can be convincingly argued that, in the sixteenth century, Geneva had no more than a partial effect on the Church of England, which was clearly Reformed but never Calvinist.

However, the uneasy compromise did not survive the political upheavals of the mid-seventeenth century, when the Puritans under the leadership of Oliver Cromwell seized the opportunity to inaugurate a Commonwealth in which Calvin's ideas were paramount. But the experiment was short-lived. Too many members of the country's ruling class were prepared to return to the more relaxed monarchical system once Cromwell was dead for it to have any chance of survival. Yet a clearly identifiable legacy remained in the various strands of religious non-conformity which subsequently grew up and played a significant part in shaping the values and attitudes that are now described as Victorian. English society was never as overtly Calvinist as Scottish society, but it was very different from the Catholic societies of southern Europe.

* Not all the English Calvinists remained in England. Many of them felt that they could not flourish within the limitations that Elizabeth and her successors imposed on them. When they left their homes they normally made for some sympathetic destination on the European mainland, such as Holland. But they were generally disappointed if they hoped to find a place that was suitable for permanent settlement. Increasing pressure on the available land meant that immigrants were less and less warmly welcomed. From the 1620s onwards the possibility of founding new settlements on the eastern seaboard of North America created considerable excitement among English and European Calvin-

ists, as well as those in exile. For the remainder of the seventeenth century the New World acted as a sanctuary for Protestants in distress. The most famous of the Calvinist settlements were those founded by the Pilgrim Fathers and their successors in New England. But it should not be forgotten that Dutch Calvinists established thriving communities in and around New Amsterdam (renamed New York when it was captured by the British). Less significant were the Huguenot settlements which tended to retain their separate identity for only a short time before they were assimilated fully into American society. The virtually independent commonwealths that the original settlers from England and Holland intended could not survive the increased interest that European governments took in North America in the eighteenth century. But communities with a strong Calvinist ethic remained in the north-east of the United States until recent times. More significantly, it is possible to identify definite strands of Calvinism within the much publicised and idealised American way of life.

6 Conclusion

Historians, interested as they are in discovering patterns in the events of the past, have naturally devoted a considerable amount of time and energy to suggesting answers to the question, 'Why was Calvinism successful in some countries and not in others?' The pattern of its geographical spread has pointed to some possible lines of inquiry. It is noticeable that all the countries in which Reformed Churches established a foothold, even on a temporary basis, were to the north of Geneva. None were to the south. Was this merely coincidence, or was there something about northern Europe that made it more receptive to Calvin's ideas? No totally convincing answers have been forthcoming, although some interesting ideas have emerged. Was it, for instance, a matter of national temperament, with the dour northern races being attracted to a creed which focused on the sinfulness and hopelessness of Man, while the sunnier Latin races did not warm to teachings that imposed strict discipline? The extent to which Calvinism spread in France would seem to cast some doubt on this hypothesis. Or was it that northern Europe lacked the political stability enjoyed by the south and was therefore more vulnerable to incursions by a revolutionary creed? Certainly many of the states in which Calvinism gained ground were suffering something of a crisis in government at the time, as were states such as Poland and Transylvania (part of modern Hungary and Rumania) in which the central government was notoriously weak. However, this theory is somewhat weakened by the fact that a number of the Italian states were equally weakly governed and yet did not succumb to Calvinism. Or was it essentially a matter of economic development, with those areas where trade and industry were flourishing and where there were large numbers of prosperous merchants and artisans being attracted to teachings which stressed the need for the individual to strive to prove his election by God, whereas states in which the economy was stagnant or in decline were likely to contain populations that were less willing to accept change? This of course would not explain the success of Calvinism among the aristocracies of some of the backward eastern European states or the lack of success in the prosperous ports of Spain and Italy.

It is obvious that none of these ideas provides a fully satisfying answer to the question. However, that does not mean that they should be dismissed out of hand. They can suggest trends that have a considerable degree of validity, as long as they are linked to a detailed consideration of the local factors applying in each case. For each country in which Calvinism made a considerable impact, it is necessary to identify the groups among whom the new ideas most extensively spread, and to explain why this was so. It is also necessary to explain why effective steps were not taken by the authorities to prevent the undermining of the existing religious arrangements, and why, in some cases, Calvinism was able to replace Catholicism as the state religion. In doing this, a number of common factors will emerge. These will undoubtedly include cultural characteristics, such as attitudes towards individualism and levels of education; political issues, especially the weakness of central government; and questions of leadership, especially among the Calvinists. The combination of factors will be different in each case, but a number of similarities will become apparent. These similarities allow historians to write meaningfully about general interpretations, while being aware that their theories can never aspire to the level of validity of scientific laws. They provide us with useful frameworks in thinking about a topic, even if they do not provide us with exact answers.

This is particularly helpful with topics such as Calvinism or the Reformation which encompass so many people about whom so little is known. It is necessary to generalise and to extrapolate from the available evidence in order to make sense of what otherwise would be a formless mass of information. But in doing so, we should be careful not to fall into the trap of imagining that the views we express have the force of objective truth. At the best of times, historical judgements are likely to be tentative to some degree: those that have to do with popular movements, especially of the distant past, are certain to be highly speculative. It is this, of course, which makes Calvin and Calvinism a potentially interesting topic of study for creative or lively minds even where there is little sympathy for the man or his message. He clearly had an enormous effect on millions of people, both in his own time and during the centuries that followed, but there is no certainty about what exactly that effect was and how exactly it was brought about. Nor is there agreement about whether his influence was to the advantage or detriment of mankind. Calvin would have argued, of course, that this

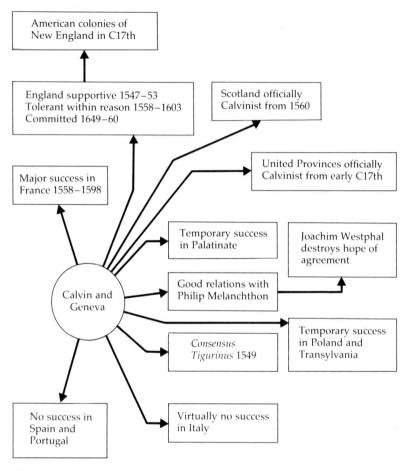

Summary – The Spread of Calvinism

was an issue that was of no concern to him for he was merely carrying out God's wishes. Not everyone would agree with him.

Making notes on 'The Spread of Calvinism'

As you make your notes on this chapter, the question you need to have in your mind throughout is, 'Why did Calvinism spread where it did and when it did?' Try to identify both those factors that were common to more than one country and those that were unique to a particular state. The following headings and questions should help you to organise your ideas.

1.   Calvin and the Protestants of Switzerland and Germany
1.1. Calvin as an independent religious leader
1.2. The *Consensus Tigurinus*. What does the *Consensus* suggest about Calvin's skill as a politician?
1.3. Dealings with the Lutherans. Why did Calvinism have so little impact on Germany?
2.   France
2.1. The political background: before 1559
2.2. The political background: after 1559
2.3. The St Bartholomew Day's Massacre. In what way was it historically significant?
2.4. 1572–1598
2.5. Reasons for Calvinism's success
3.   The Netherlands
3.1. Calvinism and rebellion
3.2. South and north. Why was Calvinism able to establish itself permanently in the northern Netherlands but not in the southern Netherlands?
3.3. Why Calvinism (rather than Lutheranism or Anabaptism)?
4.   Scotland
4.1. Background. When and why did Scotland become fertile ground for Protestantism?
4.2. John Knox
4.3. Knox and resistance to rulers
4.4. Mary Queen of Scots
4.5. The organisation of the Church. Was Knox a follower of Calvin or was he merely influenced by him?
5.   England and America
5.1. England. Why did Calvinism fail to dominate Elizabethan England?
5.2. America
6.   Conclusion. What are the possible explanations for the pattern of Calvinism's success?

Answering essay questions on 'The Spread of Calvinism'

Many of the most difficult questions on Calvin have to do with his international significance. It is not unknown to find questions that are simply worded, such as,

1. 'Examine the features of Calvinism which gave it a special appeal outside of Geneva.'

but it is much more normal to find questions of a 'challenging statement' type on this topic. And in many cases the meaning is not immediately clear. Study the following questions and work out in each case just what the questioner is expecting of you:

2. '"Calvin made the Reformation an international phenomenon." Do you agree?'
3. '"Geneva was the power house of the Calvinist Reformation." Discuss.'
4. '"Without the inspiration of John Calvin the Reformation would have been a purely temporary phenomenon." How accurate is this view?'
5. '"Suited only for backward countries and little kings." Explain this judgment of Calvinism.'
6. 'Consider the view that "The reason for the remarkable spread of Calvinism throughout sixteenth century Europe lay in its system of church government rather than in its beliefs."'

You will probably find it easiest to get into the questions if you reword them to make them more straightforward. Re-write each one, starting with either 'What?' or 'Why?' Notice that the quotation given suggests one possible answer to the question you have written. What other possible answers are there? List them. This list is the basis of your essay plan. Which 'issue' would you start with? Why? You would be well advised to devote at least a quarter (and probably a third) of the essay to the issue raised by the quotation. But never restrict your discussion to the one issue only. The question is an invitation to you to discuss the whole topic, and it is an invitation that you ignore at your peril.

Source-based questions on 'The Spread of Calvinism'

1 Knox and resistance to rulers
Read carefully the three extracts from Knox's writings given on pages 99–100. Answer the following questions:
a) What is Knox advocating in the second sentence of the first extract?
b) What justification for rebellion does Knox put forward in the second extract?
c) Why were the four propositions in the third extract thought to be so revolutionary by contemporaries?
d) In what way does Knox threaten his readers?
e) To what extent does Knox substantiate his assertions with evidence? What does this suggest about him?
f) What was the effect of Knox's writings on rulers' attitudes towards Calvinism?

2 Knox on the baptism of excommunicated people's children

Read carefully the extract from *The Book of Discipline* given on page 103. Answer the following questions:
a) What is meant by the phrase 'of age to require the same' (line 3)?
b) What argument did the author employ to justify the rule that the children of excommunicated people should not be baptised?
c) Judging by evidence within the extract, what criticism of the rule did the author expect?
d) Why did this rule arouse such controversy at the time? Why have historians considered it to be particularly significant?
e) Why did Calvinists consider discipline to be so important?

3 Calvin and Knox preaching
Study carefully the nineteenth century illustrations of Calvin (front cover) and Knox (page 101) preaching. Answer the following questions:
a) What evidence is there to support the contention that these illustrations are artists' impressions, rather than being based on first-hand experience?
b) Is the illustration of Calvin supportive of him or hostile to him? Explain your answer.
c) What impression of Knox does the artist attempt to communicate to the viewer? How does he do this?
d) Who is the woman left-centre of the Knox illustration? How is she presented?
e) What is the significance in the Knox illustration of the position and posture of the bishops?
f) Of what value are artists' impressions as historical evidence?

Further Reading

There is not a great wealth of reading available on Calvin and the later Reformation that is particularly suitable for A-level students. Undoubtedly the most helpful single piece of additional reading would be to dip into:

T. H. L. Parker, *John Calvin* (Dent 1975).

This is an academic biography, but it is very brief and generally readable. There are several discussions about disputed parts of Calvin's life that give real insights into the way in which research historians work. Time spent reading any other biographies of Calvin would not be very productive. Avoid them unless you are reading almost entirely for pleasure.

A brief summary of Calvin's life is included in:

Menna Prestwich (ed.), *International Calvinism 1541–1715* (OUP 1985).

This would make useful revision reading. The remainder of the book, with the possible exception of the chapter on 'Calvinism in France 1559–1629', is more suited to an undergraduate than to an A-level audience. Teachers will find the whole book helpful.

The most reliable work on Calvin's thinking was originally written in French, but it has long been available in English translation. It is:

F. Wendel, *Calvin: The Origins and Development of his Religious Thought* (Collins 1950).

This will seem a difficult book to all except those with a real interest in theology, but an hour spent reading one chapter would yield an increased understanding of how historians approach such topics.

You will probably come across the issue of the spread of Calvinism when you study France and The Netherlands as separate topics. Your best way into these topics will be to read Martyn Rady's two volumes in this series. These will help you to see Calvinism within the national context of the countries concerned. If you are interested in following up the issue of Calvinism in Scotland, it would probably be best to start by looking at:

Jasper Ridley, *John Knox* (OUP 1968).

This very long biography is by no means ideal as it frequently lacks direction, but it is less unreliable than most of the other works available on Knox. It is not worth spending more than an hour or two on it.

Apart from reading Parker, the most effective use of time would be to read the relevant chapters of a general history of the period in which Calvin and Calvinism are placed within the general framework of later sixteenth century international politics. Readily available is:

J. H. Elliott, *Europe Divided 1559–1598* (Fontana 1968).

It is written in an interesting and persuasive manner, and it will help tie together the various topics that you may otherwise tend to think of in isolation. Spend as much time on this book as you can afford. Your effort will not be wasted.

Sources on Calvin and the Later Reformation

One book stands out ahead of all others in offering a large amount of documentary source material on Calvin in an accessible manner. This is:

Potter and Greengrass, *John Calvin* (Edward Arnold 1983).

This paperback is excellent value for any History Department teaching the Early Modern period, although, of course, it is not to be used as a reader. It is an excellent source book.

Also valuable, although it is much less easy to make use of, is:

John Knox, *The History of the Reformation of Religion in Scotland.*

This contemporary account of events in the Scottish Reformation is available in many editions, and circulates widely in the second-hand trade. It is a rich source of very readable material that could be used in teaching the skills of handling documentary sources, especially skills relating to bias.

Acknowledgements

The publishers would like to thank the following for their permission to reproduce copyright illustrations: The Mansell Collection Limited, pages 35, 90, 101; University of Geneva, page 16 and cover.

Index